John Hewitt Jellett

The efficacy of prayer being the Donnellan lectures for the year

1877

John Hewitt Jellett

The efficacy of prayer being the Donnellan lectures for the year 1877

ISBN/EAN: 9783337278793

Printed in Europe, USA, Canada, Australia, Japan

Cover: Foto ©Lupo / pixelio.de

More available books at **www.hansebooks.com**

THE

EFFICACY OF PRAYER:

BEING

THE DONNELLAN LECTURES

FOR THE YEAR 1877.

BY

JOHN H. JELLETT, B.D.,

SENIOR FELLOW OF TRINITY COLLEGE, DUBLIN;
FORMERLY PRESIDENT OF THE ROYAL IRISH ACADEMY.

THIRD EDITION.

DUBLIN: HODGES, FOSTER, AND FIGGIS,
PUBLISHERS TO THE UNIVERSITY.
LONDON: MACMILLAN AND CO.
1880.

TO

THE REV. HUMPHREY LLOYD, D.D.,
PROVOST OF TRINITY COLLEGE, DUBLIN,

This Volume

IS, BY PERMISSION, RESPECTFULLY INSCRIBED,

BY

HIS SINCERE FRIEND,

THE AUTHOR.

PREFACE.

THERE is, I suppose, no question in Theology the decision of which more deeply affects man's practical life than this—Has Prayer any effect beyond the mind of the person who prays? If this question be answered in the negative—if we arrive at the conclusion that Prayer has no external efficacy, it is plain that its internal efficacy must speedily disappear. No man's mind can be beneficially affected by the constant repetition of that which he believes to be a mere idle form. Indeed with such a belief he would soon discontinue the practice; and it is far better that he should.

My object in the following Lectures is to examine the evidence on both sides of this important question. Previously to entering upon this examination, I have offered some remarks upon the principle which has been commonly allowed to guide such discussions. The disputant who maintains the truth of any Christian doctrine is usually expected to assume the character of an apologist—one whose duty is to *defend* the position which he has taken up; while his opponent is allowed to assume the more advantageous character of an assailant—one who has *no* position to defend, and whose sole duty is to point out any weakness which may exist in the position which he attacks. I have endeavoured to show that in practical questions, where *some* decision is inevitable, this mode of conducting the discussion is inconsistent with the principles of fair argument; giving to the advocate on the negative side of the question an advantage to which he has no just right. I have endeavoured to show, further, that this practical character attaches to the present discussion; which must therefore be conducted, not between an apologist and a critic, but between the advocates of two systems of the world, one of which includes prayer among the causes which produce or modify phenomena, while the other system excludes it.

There is another error in the discussion of questions like the present—an error which is common to the advocates on both sides of the question. It is the error of those who would decide such a question by one *kind* of evidence—according an absolute supremacy, some to statistics—some to the moral sense—some to the Bible; and treating the opposition of any other kind of evidence as a mere *difficulty*, to be explained and removed if possible; but whether explained or not, to be allowed no real weight in the decision. This mode of deciding a question is plainly illogical, unless the favoured kind of evidence has the force of demonstration—which is never the case.

I have endeavoured to guide the inquiry by the two principles here indicated—treating the question as one of comparative probability between two opposing systems of the world, and not excluding from a share in the decision *any* evidence, from whatever source derived. Lecture I. and part of Lecture II. are devoted to the establishment of these principles.

In Lectures II. and III. I have examined the class of objections to a system of the world which includes prayer, founded on the conception which the objectors have formed of the nature of God. This class of objections I have called "theological."

Lecture IV. contains an examination of a

class of objections which may be called "philosophic," being wholly independent of Theology, and professedly derived from the principles and methods of physical science.

In Lectures V. and VI. will be found the arguments on the other side of the question. In order to maintain, in accordance with the principle stated in Lecture I., an equality in form between the opposing arguments, I have stated the arguments on the positive as well as on the negative side of the question in the form of objections, pointing out the difficulties which would accompany the acceptance of a system of the world from which prayer is excluded.

Some questions, which seemed to require a more lengthened discussion than could be given to them in the text, have been examined in the Appendix. I have considered in this way the power of man to inquire into the attributes of God, and the right of the moral sense to judge of His moral attributes; the criterion of ultimate truth; the essential nature of those occurrences which we call miracles; the inherent superiority of mind over matter; the argument from statistics; and that which may be derived from the general consent of mankind.

In the Introduction I have given a brief

historical sketch of the progress of the controversy. I cannot say that the result of this investigation is satisfactory. The history itself, so far as I have been able to discover it, is very meagre. Although dating from an early period in the history of Christianity, the question of the efficacy of prayer seems to have attracted little attention for several centuries—at least I can find no trace of it, *as a controversy*, in the great Christian writers who succeeded Origen. But of course the silence of these writers does not justify us in asserting that the controversy did not then exist, though we may infer that it did not attract much notice. The same obscurity attaches to the history of the question throughout. Thus, for example, it is exceedingly difficult to determine at what time the argument against the efficacy of prayer which finds most favour in the present day—that, namely, which professes to be founded on experience—first appeared. It was certainly used early in the eighteenth century, and seems, as I have shown in the Introduction, to have been well known then. It is probable, therefore, that it was not a new argument at that time; although, with one exception, I have been unable to discover it in any of the principal writers of the century preceding.

I have only to add, that my desire throughout these Lectures was to speak as though I were addressing inquirers, and with this purpose to state the arguments fairly on both sides of the question; but with no intention, certainly, to conceal my own opinion as to the result to which such an inquiry ought to lead.

TRINITY COLLEGE,
November, 1878.

CONTENTS.

	Page.
INTRODUCTION,	xix

LECTURE I.

FUNDAMENTAL PRINCIPLE OF THE INQUIRY.

Controversy between an apologist on the one side and a critic on the other allowable in theoretical but not in practical science.—General criterion of the applicability of this form of controversy: inapplicable to many of the doctrines of Christianity.—Doctrine of the Efficacy of Prayer: its practical character.—Mode of stating the question.—Form of Theism assumed.—Divine attributes, how investigated.—Evidence of Scripture not universally applicable.—Evidence afforded by the moral faculty.— Illogical scepticism,   1-18

LECTURE II.

THEOLOGICAL ARGUMENTS AGAINST THE EFFICACY OF PRAYER.

Limitation in the use of the word "Prayer."—Has Prayer any external effect?—Question not to be decided by any one *kind* of evidence.—General statement of the theological argument against the efficacy of Prayer.—Is emotion a moral defect?—Tendency to yield to supplication justified by analysis of Prayer.—Absence of petitionary Prayer *may* show the highest faith.—Prayer considered as a condition.—Universality of moral distinctions, ... 19-35

LECTURE III.

THEOLOGICAL ARGUMENTS AGAINST THE EFFICACY OF PRAYER.—MIRACLES.

Illogical limitation of argument against miracles.—What is a miracle?—Not merely a wonder.—Essential difference of a miracle.—Causes which tend to conceal the true nature of a miracle.—Are miracles derogatory to the character of God?—Superiority of mind over matter probably perpetual.—The purposes of God may be incapable of being effected by mechanism.—Inconsistency in the limitation of the theological arguments against the Divine interference, . 36–50

LECTURE IV.

PHILOSOPHIC OBJECTIONS TO THE EFFICACY OF PRAYER.

Two opposite errors with regard to the application of arguments drawn from physical science.—General principle of Law.—Principle of Law not violated by a miracle.—No Law of Nature violated by a miracle.—Physical arguments against the efficacy of Prayer.—Method of differences.—Argument from experiment.—Hospital test.—Legitimate inference from this experiment.—Argument from statistics.—Tested by imagining the statistics to be reversed, . . . 51–69

LECTURE V.

OBJECTIONS TO A THEORY OF THE WORLD WHICH EXCLUDES PRAYER.

Argument from Scripture.—Teaching of the Old Testament.—Intercessory Prayer.—New Testament.—Teaching and example of Christ.—Argument from general consent.—Criterion of ultimate truth.—Difficulty of disbelief.—Argument from general consent cannot be altogether set aside without universal scepticism, ... 70–86

Contents. xv

LECTURE VI.

ARGUMENT AGAINST A SYSTEM OF THE WORLD WHICH
EXCLUDES PRAYER DERIVED FROM THE GENERAL ASSENT
OF MANKIND.—RECAPITULATION.

                                                                                                                             Page.

General agreement on this subject proved by the history of
Religion.—Source of this agreement a Moral Instinct.—
Man's conception of the Divine Nature, in what sense
anthropomorphic. — Argument from Christian experience. — Objection to this argument: Answer. — Objection to the criticism on the experimental test:
Answer.—Recapitulation, ...   87–103

APPENDIX.

Note A, Page 1.

IMPOSSIBILITY OF MAINTAINING A SCEPTICAL ATTITUDE WITH
REGARD TO RELIGION.

Bishop Butler's decision of this question.—Reservation
with which it is to be understood, ...   105–6

Note B, Page 8.

OBJECTIONS TO A STATEMENT OF THE QUESTION AS TO LYING
BETWEEN OPPOSING PROBABILITIES.

This statement may seem unduly favourable to the negative side.—Principle of Bishop Butler.—Injurious effects
of a delusive belief in the efficacy of Prayer, ...   106–9

Note C, Page 13.

ATTRIBUTES OF THE DEITY.

Can man form any conception of the Divine attributes?—
Opinion of Mr. Herbert Spencer.—Meaning of "The
Absolute" as applied to the Divine Being.—Ambiguity

of the word "unknowable."—In what sense is it true that it is unphilosophic to inquire into "the unknowable"?—Not true as applied to an inquiry into the Divine attributes.—Utility of such inquiry.—Effect which would be produced on the religious sentiment if the inquiry were wholly renounced, ...   109–21

NOTE D, PAGE 15.
CRITERION OF ULTIMATE TRUTH.

Belief in our criterion of truth.—Impossibility of disbelief to be preferred to belief as a criterion of truth.—Ambiguity in the expression "impossibility of disbelief."—Difference between "incredible" and "inconceivable."—The test of truth is the *incredibility*, not the *inconceivability*, of the opposite.—Principle of causation.—Mr. Spencer's use of the word "unbelievable."—Is it admissible?—Example.—*Difficulty* not *impossibility* of disbelief the general criterion of truth, ...   122–41

NOTE E, PAGE 17.
RIGHT OF THE MORAL FACULTY TO JUDGE OF THE ATTRIBUTES OF GOD.

Answer to the question given by Mansel.—Different answer given by F. W. Newman.—Those who deny the right are bound to disprove it.—Effect of the denial on revealed religion.—Moral sense not infallible.—Errors of the intellect often attributed to the moral sense.—Decision of the moral sense often given upon an imaginary case, for which the intellect is responsible.—Instance in the Calvinistic controversy.—Assumed infallibility of Scriptural evidence.—Mr. Mansel's definition of "moral miracles."—Is the moral law ever suspended?. . . .   141–52

NOTE F, PAGE 23.
OBJECTIONS TO PRAYER DERIVED FROM THE REGULAR SEQUENCE OF PHENOMENA.

Natural law violated by the success of Prayer for a physical benefit, according to Mr. Stopford Brooke.—Is this true?—Effect of the voluntary actions of men.—Instance in the rainfall, ...   152–5

Note G, Page 25.

IS AN EMOTION A MORAL DEFECT?

Answer to the question given by the Stoical philosophy.—Rejected by the general sense of mankind.—Is the absence of emotion in a higher order of beings a mark of their superiority?—Opinion of Bishop Butler.—Do we consider the moral character to be exalted by the insensibility which is often produced, even in the benevolent, by familiarity with scenes of sorrow?—Is the Divine mind wholly without passive power?—Dilemma, . . .   156–61

Note H, Page 38.

WHAT IS A MIRACLE?

Opinion of Professor Mansel—Professor Baden Powell—Bishop Butler.—Archbishop Trench.—Two *laws* cannot be opposed.—Is the difficulty of admitting the truth of a miracle lessened by the principle that "God works by means"?—Opinion of the Duke of Argyll.—Instance in the plague of locusts, ...   161–8

Note I, Page 41.

ILLOGICAL DISTINCTION BETWEEN THE WORLD OF SPIRIT AND THE WORLD OF MATTER.

Argument of the Duke of Argyll against this distinction, .   169

Note K, Page 46.

INHERENT SUPERIORITY OF MIND OVER MATTER.

This superiority may be asserted without deciding the question whether mind and matter be modifications of the same substance.—Marks of superiority.—Power of invention. Power of improvement.—Man could not be fully replaced by a machine.—Is this a defect in man? .   169–73

NOTE L, PAGE 68.

THE STATISTICAL ARGUMENT.

Page.

Opposite opinions as to the applicability of the statistical argument.—Dr. Hessey.—Mr. Galton.—The statistical argument is applicable, but has no right to a monopoly.—Principle laid down by Mr. Galton for the guidance of the statistical inquiry.—Statistics collected on this principle inapplicable to the Christian theory of Prayer.—Two elements of uncertainty in arguments derived from statistics of recovery from sickness.—Argument from the silence of physicians with regard to the efficacy of Prayer.—This would prove too much.—Assumption made by Mr. Galton in the construction of the statistical argument.—Instances.—Length of life of kings.—Of the clergy.—Differently treated by Mr. Galton.—Logical conditions of the Method of Differences.—General conclusion, ... 174–88

NOTE M, PAGE 79.

ARGUMENT FROM THE GENERAL CONSENT OF MANKIND.

Ought any weight to be attached to the belief of others?—Relation between this question and that of the criterion of ultimate truth.—Sole use of the argument from other people's opinions, according to Mill.—Logical consequence of this principle.—This principle is seldom or never logically carried out, but such a development is not impossible.—Presumption in favour of the truth of the thing believed. First question to be asked in determining the value of such belief. Case of intuitive beliefs.—Moral intuitions.—Application to the question of the efficacy of Prayer.—Mr. Galton's *reductio ad absurdum* of the argument from universality.—It is not an absurdity that the prayer of a heathen may meet with favour, . . . 188–203

INTRODUCTION.

AMONG the subjects of controversy which engaged the attention of pre-Christian Theists, the Efficacy of Prayer can hardly be reckoned. Whether a God or Gods existed, and what was their nature—whether they were corporeal or incorporeal, mortal or immortal—these were questions which possessed a certain amount of interest. But the efficacy of prayer to these deities does not seem to have been, directly, a subject of discussion. With, at least, the great majority of pre-Christian Theists, this dogma seems to have been regarded as a necessary part of Theism. That the God, or Gods, whose existence they admitted, were quite as properly objects of prayer as of any other kind of worship, and that these beings were influenced by the prayers of their worshippers, were articles of belief nearly co-extensive with the belief in the existence of the deities themselves. Plato puts into the mouth of Socrates a warning against rash or ignorant prayer, but the danger from which he would guard Alcibiades is that his prayer may be granted, not that it may be refused.[1] Cicero, who has treated largely of the existence, nature, and providence of the Gods, gives no indication of any scepticism among Theists as to the efficacy of prayer.

There is indeed an apparent exception to the truth of the statement that no pre-Christian Theists were sceptical on this subject. An Epicurean would not, probably, have called himself an Atheist, yet his Theism was such as to render this belief impossible. Prayer to a being who was supposed to take no part in human affairs—nay, from whose existence all activity was supposed to be absent, could only be a mockery. Nor indeed is the applicability of this remark limited to the theology of Epicurus. *Any* theology which denies the *present* activity of the Divine Being renders prayer an absurdity. So far as this question is concerned, it matters not whether, with the Epicurean, we suppose the Deity to have been *always* inactive, or assume, with some modern thinkers, that He, as it were, "set the universe going," and then abandoned it to the action of secondary causes.

In a certain sense, therefore, the controversy with regard to the efficacy of prayer may be said to have existed among

[1] *Alcibiades* II.

ancient Theists. But it can hardly be said to have had a separate existence. It was merged in the more general question of the nature of the Gods. We may not say that the efficacy of prayer was admitted by *all* ancient Theists, but it does seem that this doctrine was not denied by any whose theology rendered its admission possible. Even with Epicurus and his followers, the denial of the efficacy of prayer is to be inferred rather from the nature of their theology than from any distinct statement. Cotta, arguing as an Academic, alleges as a *reductio ad absurdum* of Epicureanism, that it renders prayer nugatory.[1]

There is some difficulty in ascertaining with precision the opinion of the Stoics on this subject. If this opinion be deduced from the system of the world taught by Zeno, Chrysippus, and their followers, it might seem that no efficacy could have been attributed to prayer. For prayer can hardly exist under a system of either Pantheism or Fatalism, and the Stoical doctrine appears to have partaken of both characters. Pantheism which denies the personality of the Divine Being, and Fatalism which supposes the sequence of events to be fixed beyond the power of God or man to change—both these theories seem to exclude prayer. On the other hand, the propriety of prayer was distinctly taught by members of the Stoic school.

[1] Cicero, *de Natura Deorum*, lib. i. c. 44.

Diogenes Laertius, in enumerating the dogmas of the Stoic philosophy, says—"The wise man will pray, asking good things from the Gods, as Posidonius says in the first book of his treatise on Duties, and Hecaton says the same thing in the thirteenth book of his treatise on Extraordinary Things."[1] It is remarkable that Posidonius is mentioned by the same author as one of those Stoics who taught that all things were produced by fate.[2] It would seem therefore that the Stoics had some way of reconciling these apparently inconsistent theories, or perhaps that they did not perceive the inconsistency. Moreover, the doctrine that the world is ruled by a power independent of the Gods was certainly not held by all the members of the Stoic School. Balbus, introduced by Cicero as the representative of the Stoics, distinctly states their belief that the world is ruled "by the providence *of the Gods*"; complaining that the Epicureans misrepresented them by omitting the words "of the Gods," and thus making them, as it were, personify Providence as a distinct power ("tanquam anum fatidicam"). These words were, he says, omitted by the Stoics merely for the sake of brevity, and were always understood.[3] On the whole, I do not

---

[1] Diogenes Laertius (Yonge's translation), p. 304.
[2] *Ib.* p. 313.
[3] Cicero, *de Natura Deorum*, lib. ii. § 29.

Introduction. xxiii

think that we should be justified in describing the Stoics as unbelievers in the efficacy of prayer, however this scepticism might seem to be the necessary result of their philosophic tenets.

There is another fact which it is necessary to notice, inasmuch as it may seem to be inconsistent with the assertion that the efficacy of prayer was accepted by all the pre-Christian Theists, whose theology rendered such a belief possible. Speaking of the denial of this doctrine by Prodicus and his followers, Clement of Alexandria tells them that they must not imagine themselves to be original in this scepticism, which had characterised, long before, the philosophers of the Cyrenaic School.[1] Elsewhere Clement defends Theodorus, one of the most distinguished disciples of this School, against the charge of Atheism, which had been very freely brought against him.[2] If we may rely on Clement in both his statements, it would seem that we have here an instance of pre-Christian Theists who denied the efficacy of prayer, and of whom we have no proof that their theology rendered belief in this doctrine impossible.

With regard to Clement's defence of Theodorus, it is in

---

[1] Vol. ii., p. 415 (Clark's *Ante-Nicene Christian Library*).
[2] Vol. i., p. 33. For the charge of Atheism *vide* Cicero, *de Natura Deorum*, lib. i. § 42.

truth rather a confirmation than a refutation of the charge of Atheism—amounting in fact to this, that Theodorus had renounced the false theology of his time, yet without acquiring anything better. No account remains to us of the Cyrenaic theology—if they had a theology. They have left no authoritative record of their system, and we are obliged to have recourse to such information as we can gather from authors who wrote long after the school had ceased to exist. From Diogenes Laertius, who has left us the most detailed account of the Cyrenaic philosophy, we learn their opinions on many physical and ethical questions; but only one doubtful phrase is capable of a theological reference. Among the qualities from which a wise man ought to be free, the Cyrenaics reckoned one which may be either religious or superstitious according to the meaning which we assign to the Greek word used (δεισιδαιμονία).[1] If the former be the true meaning, it would go far to justify the accusation of Atheism which has been brought against them. If we are to understand the word in the second sense, it would leave the question of the nature or existence of Cyrenaic theology undecided. On the whole, if this School had any definite maxim on the sub-

---

[1] Lib. ii., segm. 91, 92. The reason given for the freedom of the wise man from δεισιδαιμονία, namely, that this quality is the result of an unreal notion (κενὴν δόξαν), would apply to either sense of the word.

Introduction. xxv

ject of prayer, such a maxim may have arisen, not improbably, from the absence of, at least, practical Theism. Certainly the *ethical* system of Aristippus breathes very little piety.

The first systematic discussion of this question which I have been able to discover is contained in the writings of Maximus Tyrius, about the middle of the second century. His eleventh dissertation bears the title, "Whether prayer is right" (εἰ δεῖ εὔχεσθαι)—a question which he decides in the negative. His argument is not unlike that afterwards ascribed by Origen to the sceptics of his own time. Maximus Tyrius contends that if those who pray are worthy to gain their petitions, they will gain them without prayer; nay, all the more because they will have shown (by not praying) both modesty and faith.[1] Further, in opposition to prayer for individual benefits, he argues that if events are arranged by the Divine Providence, and if this Providence concerns itself, as he thinks probable, only about the general interest, private petitions will not be granted.[2]

The controversy as to the duty and efficacy of prayer found a very early place in the history of Christianity. In the treatise[3] which Origen has devoted to the subject of

[1] Dissertation xi. p. 117 (Davis's edition).
[2] *Ib.* p. 118.
[3] Tom. i. p. 186, *et seq.* (Benedictine edition).

prayer, is to be found the statement of objections which are alleged by the controversialists of the present day. There is, for example, no one of the *theological*[1] objections against the efficacy of prayer more commonly urged by modern controversialists than this dilemma—If it be *right* that we should have the blessing for which we pray, God will grant it to us without prayer, and if it be not right, He will not grant it at all. This objection is stated and commented on by Origen.[2] Other objections equally familiar to us now are stated by the same author. Thus, for example, it is objected to prayer for virtue that, if the petitioner be one of the elect, he will gain his object without prayer, and if he be not one of the elect, he will not attain it by prayer.[3] This dilemma resembles the former, showing however by its form of expression that it was derived from a source professedly Christian. The same is indeed apparently true of all the objections enumerated by Origen, who does not seem to concern himself with non-Christian disputants. We may add to those already mentioned the ordinary objections derived from the unchangeability and foreknowledge of God, which are also stated and discussed by Origen.[4]

If Origen's account of the class of men from whom ob-

[1] *Infra*, p. 22.
[2] Tom. i., p. 205.
[3] Tom. i., p. 204.
[4] *Ib.* pp. 206–8.

jections to prayer proceeded be true, there is a certain similarity between the sceptics of his time and those already alluded to as belonging to an earlier period. With the later sceptics, as with the Epicureans, denial of the efficacy of prayer, if we are to accept the statement of Origen, would appear to have been a necessary result of their fundamental principles. The Epicurean *could* not admit that prayer had any effect with deities whom he believed to be wholly inactive. And according to Origen, denial of its efficacy was almost entirely confined to those who disbelieved, although they might not openly deny, either the existence or the providence of God.[1] To both these classes—the Atheist and the Epicurean—the efficacy of prayer was obviously an absurdity. But it must be admitted that the objections against this doctrine enumerated by Origen do not, when considered in themselves, appear to have been founded upon either Atheistical or Epicurean principles. The objectors may indeed have thought it advisable to argue rather upon the principles of their opponents than upon their own; but the internal

---

[1] Tom. i. p. 203. This is the only consistent meaning which I can put upon two apparently contradictory statements of Origen—one, that scarcely any one denied the efficacy of prayer who did not also reject either the existence or the providence of God; the other, that he does not propose to consider the objections made by any person who rejected either of these doctrines.

evidence, so far as it goes, seems to be unfavourable to the truth of Origen's statement. It appears to be more probable that, then as now, there existed a class of men who, believing in the existence and providence of God, rejected the doctrine of the efficacy of prayer, principally because they found it to be inconsistent with their theistic conceptions. Among Pagan Theists, Maximus Tyrius appears to have belonged to this class.

Of the sect founded by Prodicus, to which Clement attributes disbelief in the efficacy of prayer, we have no minute information. It was probably an offshoot of the Carpocratians, a sect of Alexandrian Gnostics which existed in the second century. Whether Prodicus inherited from them this particular opinion we do not know; probably, however, had the fact been so, Clement would have recorded it.

Combining these several facts—1. That of the Christian writers of the second century only the two Alexandrians, Clement and Origen, allude to this controversy; 2. That the denial of the efficacy of prayer is attributed by Clement to Prodicus, a Gnostic and probably a disciple of the Alexandrian Carpocrates; 3. That the first distinct statement of the controversy is to be found in the writings of Maximus Tyrius, who, although not an Alexandrian, was a Platonic philosopher—we may infer with probabi-

Introduction. xxix

lity that its source is to be sought in the Neo-Platonic School of Alexandria. If this be true, we may fix the date of its commencement at some period between A.D. 100 and A.D. 150. No allusion to it is to be found in the works of the Platonist Philo; and his silence renders it improbable that it was known in the first century. On the other hand, it is distinctly stated by Maximus Tyrius, who was at the zenith of his fame under Marcus Aurelius, A.D. 161-80.

So far as we can judge from the principal Christian writers, the controversy appears to have slumbered for many centuries after the time of Origen. Chrysostom and Augustine have both dwelt largely upon the subject of prayer, and the same is true in different degrees of Cyril, Hilary, and others. But no one of these writers appears to be conscious of the existence of any general scepticism as to its efficacy. They notice, indeed, and labour to remove, certain difficulties which are opposed to the acceptance of this doctrine. Thus, for example, the question—why, in answer to human prayer, the blessing prayed for often comes but slowly, is quite a favourite subject of discussion; as is also the reconcilement of the efficacy of prayer with the Divine foreknowledge. But the tone of these writers is that of teachers rather than that of controversialists. They write, apparently, more with the purpose of removing difficulties from the minds of believers than with the purpose of convincing or confuting unbelievers. It is of course impossible to say that the controversy did not exist. It undoubtedly did exist in the time of Origen, and probably continued to exist subsequently, although I have been unable to trace it. But the silence of such writers as Chrysostom and Augustine with respect to this controversy justifies the supposition that it was not very conspicuous, or perhaps not very widely diffused.

In the writings of Thomas Aquinas (second half of the thirteenth century) the question assumes a definitely controversial shape. Difficulties attendant on the theory of prayer are noticed and treated of, not as perplexities felt by believers, but as objections alleged by opponents. Like the objections noticed by Origen, and indeed *all* the early objections to the efficacy of prayer, the arguments stated and controverted by Thomas Aquinas are of the kind which I have called theological.[1] Some are founded on the prescience or the immutability of God.[2] One depends on the assumed principle, that, as it is a stronger proof of liberality to give unasked than in compliance with a petition, the offering of such a petition is an affront to Him.[3] Another is founded on the theory of

[1] *Infra*, p. 22.   [2] Part ii., div. ii., qu. 83, art. 2.   [3] *Ibid.*

Introduction. xxxi

predestination.¹ Another, which is indeed rather moral than theological, deprecates prayer for temporal blessings, because anxiety for such things lowers the tone of the mind, and is moreover forbidden to us.²

The history so far, and indeed for a long period after the time of Thomas Aquinas, is, as I have said, that of a controversy purely theological. The objectors of the thirteenth century, like the objectors of the second century, derive their arguments against the efficacy of prayer from its supposed inconsistency with the Divine attributes. There is as yet no trace (so far at least as I can discover) of the arguments, so popular in our day, derived from the principles and methods of physical science. Nor is this to be wondered at. Physical science can hardly be said to have existed. The methods of physical science, in the modern sense of those words, did not exist. We can therefore hardly expect to find arguments such as these in use before the time of Bacon.

That Bacon himself had no scepticism with regard to the efficacy of prayer, even in the physical world, appears from one of the prayers which he has left behind—prayers evidently composed for his own use. This prayer contains a distinct petition for a temporal blessing—"O Lord, let thy holy angels pitch their tents about us, to

¹ Part i., qu. 23, art. 8. ² Part ii., div. ii., qu. 83, art. 6.

guard and defend us from all the malice of Satan, and from all perils both of soul *and body*."[1] I cannot find that he has treated of the question itself.

I can discover no proof that this controversy obtained much attention during the seventeenth century. The great English divines of that time have hardly noticed it. Among the philosophic writers, Hobbes defends the practice of prayer, not because it influences the Divine will, but because it is the condition which God has prescribed to those who desire to obtain His blessings.[2] At the close of this century, however (A.D. 1695), Bayle notices an objection to which, since his time, much importance has been attached, namely, that, as a matter of fact, devout prayers are not always granted.[3] But he does not go so far as to say that they are *never* granted. In other words, although denying that devout prayer is *always* efficacious, he does not assert that it is *never* efficacious. It is remarkable that Bayle admits, as a matter of fact, that the arguments on the positive side of this question generally produce in the minds of those who hear or read them a conviction which is almost complete.[4]

[1] Vol. vii. pp. 7, 8 (Montague's edition).
[2] *Opera Philosophica*, vol. ii. p. 124 (Molesworth's edition).
[3] *Dict. Hist. et Crit.*, tom. iv. p. 235 (5th edition). *Art. Sommono-Codom*.
[4] *Ibid.*

Introduction. xxxiii

The argument thus briefly noticed by Bayle is mentioned and controverted by Wollaston;[1] who alleges in opposition to it the uncertainty which necessarily attends the attempt to discover the effects of prayer from actual observation, with other arguments which have been often used since. Some years later the same objection is adopted by Chubb.[2] It is remarkable that, in the development of this objection, Chubb adduces the same case upon which Mr. Galton has laid great stress, namely, the want of success which attends prayer for kings. There is however this difference—that, whereas Mr. Galton's argument is founded on the alleged failure of prayer for the longevity of kings, Chubb's argument is founded on the alleged failure of prayer for their morality.

The argument against the efficacy of prayer derived from the supposed invariability of the course of Nature probably took its rise about the same time. It is not noticed by Bayle, but Dr. Samuel Clarke early in the eighteenth century speaks of it as being commonly known then. In his sermon on the Duty of Prayer (Serm. CLVIII.), after urging the necessity of faith as a condition of successful prayer, he says—" The greatest objection that vain men have made against the faith I am

[1] *Religion of Nature,* p. 125.
[2] *Posthumous Works,* vol. i., pp. 279-80.

speaking of is, that things seem regularly to proceed in the course of Nature, and according to the efficiency of second causes; and that therefore, 'What is the Almighty that we should serve him? and what profit should we have if we pray unto Him?'"—Job. xxi. 15.[1]

No substantial change in the lines of the controversy appears to have been made since the early part of the eighteenth century. Arguments have been indeed worked out in greater detail, and in one case an important modification has been suggested; but in principle these arguments have remained the same. Inconsistency with the character of God—inconsistency with the laws of Nature—inconsistency with experience—these were the objections alleged early in the eighteenth century against the supposition of the Divine interference, and these are the objections urged still. The present state of the controversy may be gathered very fully from several papers which appeared in the Contemporary and Fortnightly Reviews for the years 1872-3, by Professor Tyndall, Mr. Galton, Professor M'Cosh, Mr. Littledale, Mr. Knight, the Duke of Argyll, and an anonymous writer to whom I shall allude presently. The arguments on the negative side of the question are founded on the three principles which I have stated, and so far they cannot be said to involve anything new.

[1] *Works*, vol. ii., p. 281.

Introduction.

But the modern controversy, though not new in its principles, is marked by certain features which are peculiar to itself. It is less Theistic than the older controversies. Some of the disputants, setting the theological arguments wholly aside, have assumed the right to decide the question by the methods of physical science—observation and experiment; the use of this latter method having been suggested (I believe for the first time) by the anonymous writer to whom I have before alluded.

Among the theological arguments which are thus set aside, none are excluded more rigorously than those derived from Scripture. In discussing the kindred question of miracles, Spinoza has taken some trouble to prove that Scripture is on his side.[1] I do not suppose that any modern controversialist, holding the opinions of Spinoza, would do as much. Certainly if we take our ideas of modern thought from the controversy of 1872-3, we shall be inclined to think that the evidence of Scripture has been altogether banished from the discussion. Indeed the assertion of Mr. Galton that "the collapse of the argument of universality leaves us solely concerned with a simple statistical question"[2] can mean no less. The tacit refusal of the disputants on one side of the question to argue it,

---

[1] *Tractatus Theologico-Politicus*, cap. vi.
[2] *Fortnightly Review*, vol. xii. (new series), p. 126.

in any degree, upon Scriptural evidence seems to have widened the separation between them and some of the disputants on the positive side; while others, anxious to preserve some common ground, have been perhaps too ready to fight the whole battle upon a field chosen by their opponents. Thus the controversy has become less Theistic. But indeed this tendency to decide a question, not by a review of the *whole* evidence, but by that kind only which the reasoner's habits of thought have led him to prefer, is not peculiar to the controversies of theology.

The controversy of 1872-3 is also marked by an attempt to define a certain sphere within which prayer *is* efficacious—excluding it strictly from the world of matter, but conceding to it a very large power in the world of spirit. This species of compromise would, no doubt, neutralise objections which have been made to the doctrine in the name of physical science. But I think that few persons, having read Mr. Knight's two papers,[1] and the reply of the Duke of Argyll[1] to the first, will think that the attempt was successful. I may add that, although this limitation of the sphere in which the efficacy of prayer is asserted would relieve the doctrine from the statistical objection as stated by Mr. Galton, it would not relieve it from the statistical objection as stated by Chubb (p. xxxi).

[1] *Contemporary Review*, vols. xxi., xxiii.

Introduction. xxxvii

The prayers of their subjects could have no effect, according to Mr Knight, in increasing the *longevity* of kings, but there is no reason why such prayers should not be efficacious in improving their *morality*.

To any person who reviews calmly the present state of the controversy, it must be a matter of deep regret that into this, as into so many theological discussions, there has been infused a spirit of bitterness highly unfavourable to the cause of truth. Writers on the negative side of this great question complain, that accusations have been brought against them and injurious epithets applied to them, which they are conscious to themselves that they do not merit. Unfortunately this is not a solitary case. The *odium theologicum* has passed into a proverb; and it has become usual to contrast the passion and bitterness of theologians with the philosophic calm of scientific men, greatly to the disadvantage of the former. But the comparison is not just; and there is something to be said in apology for this violence, cruel and disastrous as it has often been. The scientific man is calm—true; but he has usually no temptation to be otherwise. His happiness is in nowise involved in the result of the investigation which he conducts; and he may therefore bring to his task a mind unprejudiced and unimpassioned—earnest for truth, and having no reason to be earnest for anything else. But, while human nature is what it is, it would be vain to expect that men will bring the same tranquillity to a discussion in whose result their hopes and affections are deeply concerned. So it is with many of the discussions of theology; and in an eminent degree with the doctrine which forms our present subject.

True or untrue, the doctrine of the efficacy of prayer has been to millions the very life-blood of their religion. It is associated with the affections of their earliest childhood. It has accompanied them in the struggles of maturer life. In pain and in sorrow it has been their comfort to think that there is a Friend of whom they may ask relief with a hope that the prayer will be successful. The comfort may be a delusion—the hope utterly baseless; and if this be so, it is the duty of those who see more clearly to show to their weaker brethren that they are deceived by a phantom. But when we expect that men will receive the attempt to destroy one of their dearest hopes with the equanimity which marks the student of pure science, we are asking of human nature more than it can give. Perfect allegiance to truth does indeed require that we should weigh with complete impartiality the evidence by which an asserted doctrine is sustained, how long and closely soever it may have twined itself into our hearts. So, too, does a perfect allegiance to truth require that we should weigh with complete impartiality the evidence by which a criminal charge is sustained, regardless of the fact that the accused is our dearest friend. But human nature cannot do it.

It is, I repeat, vain to expect that a contest in which men's affections are engaged can be carried on with the tranquillity which characterizes the discussions of pure science. It is not so in the contests of politics—it is not so in the contests of theology; and it is scarcely possible that it should ever be so. But the disputants would do well to remember that the advocate whose words are to be *read* cannot use bitter and passionate language with the same effect, nor even with the same impunity, as the advocate whose words are only to be *heard*. Did the Christian advocate always bear in mind how much *his* cause, above all others, is injured by the use of language of this kind, we should probably hear less of it in theological controversy.

There *are* attacks directed against the Christian religion which cannot and ought not to be met by a purely intellectual opposition. Sneers against that which men venerate, like sneers against those whom they love, must excite in their minds a feeling of moral reprobation—contempt, if these sneers are powerless—indignation, if they affect the minds of other men. But there are attacks, and those the most formidable of all, which cannot be met with these weapons. The Christian advocate would do well to remember that, in the world of educated men, he has no opponent so dangerous as the respectful sceptic; who, refusing to believe, gives without passion the reasons for his unbelief. Such an opponent is not to be met by invective; and he who chooses this weapon must be prepared for the inference, that he has chosen it because in a contest of reason he could only expect defeat. Probably no cause has suffered more from this inference than the cause of Christianity.

LECTURE I.

FUNDAMENTAL PRINCIPLES OF THE INQUIRY.

St. Luke, ix. 50.

"He that is not against us is for us."

St. Matth. xii. 30.

" He that is not with me is against me."

THE two passages which I have here quoted might, to a hasty reader, present an appearance of incongruity. In reality, they are but different expressions of the same truth—the impossibility, namely, of maintaining a neutral attitude towards religion. Limited in expression here to the religion of Christ, they really enunciate a principle applicable to all religions. They tell us that it is impossible to maintain a purely sceptical attitude with regard to Christianity; and that is true, not because it is *Christianity*, but because it is a *religion*— because it is not a mere system of speculative truth, but is intended to influence the lives of men.[1]

[1] Appendix, Note A.

I have prefixed these passages to the investigation in which I have now to engage you, as indicating concisely the principle on which I propose to conduct it—a principle not peculiar to the present question, but which ought to underlie all such investigations. This principle I now proceed to state more fully.

The word "apologist," so commonly applied to those who have written favourably of the evidence of Christianity, expresses a disadvantageous position, which has been very generally assigned to them, and which they have been, I think, too ready to accept. If of two controversialists the one is required to assume a position purely defensive, while the other is permitted to assume a position purely critical, there can be no doubt that the second controversialist starts with an enormous advantage. Not, be it observed, necessarily an unfair advantage. There are controversies in which the rules of right reason absolutely require those who conduct them to assume this relative position. There are controversies which, from their very nature, must be conducted between critics on the one side and defenders, or, to use our former term, apologists, on the other. Still, I repeat, in any such controversy, the disputant who is allowed to assume the position of a mere critic enjoys an immense advantage. He is not expected to prove anything. He is not required to show that the position which he defends is stronger than that occupied by his opponent, for he defends no position. His duty is simply to criticise the argument of his opponent; to point out its weakness, if it have any such; to show (and this more nearly concerns our present inquiry) that there are difficulties which his opponent has failed to remove—to show, in fact, that the argument which he criticises falls short of full proof. In a word, the apologist is required to prove his assertion to be true, while the critic is not required to prove it to be untrue. If the apologist fail to do that which is thus required of him, the critic has but to point out the failure, and he will be pronounced to have been victorious.

Now, there are controversies in which this is quite right, but there are controversies in which it is wholly wrong; and as the controversial principle which I have stated gives necessarily to one of the supposed disputants a very serious advantage, it is right that before such a principle is adopted we should seek to define the class of questions to which it is applicable, in order that we may determine whether in this class the controversy in hand be included.

Now, in the first place, it is quite plain that there *is* such a class. In the scientific world we know it well. Thus, when a scientific man is presented with a theory of any natural phenomenon, he is in general perfectly justified in assuming a position purely critical. It is in general his undoubted right to criticise the theory which is submitted to him; to state any scientific objections which may be alleged against it; to point out any parts of the complex phenomenon which it has failed to account for; and that without being required to advance any theory of his own. This is perfectly just, so long as we have to deal with purely theoretical science. You may refuse to believe that light is an undulation without being required to maintain that it is a projectile, or to hold any theory on the subject; and you may do this because in such a question the mind may, after hearing the evidence, reasonably assume any one of three attitudes—namely, belief, disbelief, or unbelief. But let the question pass from the region of theory to the region of practice, and the third of these attitudes usually becomes impossible. If the question which the theory professes to solve be a practical one, you cannot usually take up the position of unbelief. You may act as if you believed the theory to be true, or you may act as if you believed it to be false; but you cannot act as if you did not know whether it be true or false. So far as your actions are concerned, you cannot leave the question undecided.

A single example taken from the world of science will sufficiently illustrate this principle. The physicist, who believes in the nearly spherical figure of the Earth, is bound to maintain his thesis against all comers, without being entitled to require of any objector that he should produce a counter-theory. If he attempt to meet an objection by asking of the objector, "Well, what do you believe the Earth's figure to be?" the other may fairly retort—"I do not know—I have no theory on the subject, and am merely exercising my right to criticise yours."

But this retort, perfectly fair when addressed to a physicist, would have no force at all if addressed to a sailor. For *he* may quite fairly reply—"Then I cannot listen to you. I must decide the question; the exigencies of my profession require that I should decide it. I must have charts; I must be guided by rules of navigation; and neither charts nor rules can be constructed without answering the question—'What is the figure of the Earth?' That which I have to determine, therefore, is not whether the received theory be free from all objections, but whether it be more probable than any other theory which has been started. Scepticism may be possible to you—it is impossible to me."

The principle contained in this answer indicates exactly the inquiry which we ought to make before we allow a controversy to be conducted as between an apologist on one side, and a critic on the other:—Is the question at issue of such a kind that the mind may refuse to come to *any* decision? is an attitude of pure scepticism possible? If it be, then the mere critic has a legitimate standing ground, and this mode of conducting the controversy is legitimate too. If it be not, the position of the mere critic is untenable, and the mode of conducting the controversy of which I have spoken should not be permitted by the apologist, if he desire to do justice to his cause.

We have now to inquire to which of these classes religious controversy—and more especially that question which is now to engage us—properly belongs. How far is it right that the Christian apologist should concede to his opponent the position of a mere critic? Applying the test which has just been defined, we must inquire—Is it possible to maintain, with regard to Christian doctrines, an attitude purely sceptical? Now there are doctrines very commonly included in systems of Christianity, with regard to which it is quite possible to maintain this attitude. Take, for example, the doctrine of the eternity of future punishment. You are not compelled to decide that question; for whether you believe the doctrine to be true, or believe it to be false, or leave the question undecided, your life and actions may be quite the same. And therefore the opponent of such a doctrine as this may quite justly take up a purely critical position, refusing to decide the question at all, until the evidence, on one side or the other, attains a considerable preponderance.

But there are parts of Christianity with regard to which you could not assume such an attitude. Take, for example, the doctrine of Theism itself, at least as Christians understand it. The truth of that doctrine is a question which you cannot leave undecided, by your life, if not by your words. You may say, as Positivists do say, that you do not know whether there is a God or no; but you must *live* either as a Theist or as an Atheist; and, therefore, I conceive, the Theist who allows his opponent to assume a position purely critical, maintaining himself a position purely defensive, makes a concession injurious to his cause, and forbidden by the rules of just reasoning. The question which man's life requires him to decide is not whether the existence of a God be proved by overwhelming evidence, but whether the scheme of Theism or of Atheism—a system of the world which includes the Divine element, or a system of the world which excludes it—be the more probable. For according to one or other of these systems you must live. If you say, as some do say, "The evidence is not satisfactory, and I must therefore decline to decide the question," you profess to do that which you cannot do. Your life will decide it. You may imagine your attitude to be one of philosophic scepticism —practically it is an attitude of disbelief; and if you assume this attitude in the face of *any* preponderance of evidence in favour of the system of Theism as opposed to the system of Atheism, then, I conceive, your conduct is not consistent with the principles of just reason.

Having thus indicated these two classes of truth—the class, namely, towards which the mind can, and the class towards which it cannot, maintain a sceptical attitude—I proceed now to inquire to which of these classes the doctrine which is to form the subject of the present Course of Lectures properly belongs—I mean the doctrine of the efficacy of prayer. And, in the first place, let me state the doctrine itself, as I propose to consider it.

The doctrine of the efficacy of prayer, which is a part, though not a necessary part, of Theism, asserts that among the causes which produce or modify phenomena, both mental and physical, prayer is one. It asserts that this effect is produced, not as in the case of causes purely physical, by necessary consequence, but through the intervention of the will of the Supreme Being in the series of antecedents. It asserts, therefore, by necessary implication, that the will of the Supreme Being is a real cause—a cause whose action is not confined to the past, when it may be supposed to have called into existence certain forces which were destined thenceforward to act by themselves, but active *now*, intervening *now* in the sequence of physical phenomena, in a manner analogous to the intervention of man, or any other personal being, in a similar series. It asserts that the Supreme Being has prescribed to man, as the means of obtaining this interference, prayer. It does not assert that this means is absolutely necessary, nor does it promise unfailing success.

But it does assert that among the antecedents which determine the Divine interference, prayer is one. It asserts that this connexion is of Divine appointment, and that therefore it is the duty of man to make use of the means so ordained.

Now, it seems plain that this doctrine belongs to that practical class just described, towards which we cannot, in our lives, assume a sceptical attitude. We must either pray, or abstain from prayer. If we pray, we act as if the doctrine were true. If we abstain from prayer, we act as if the doctrine were false; that is to say, we act in the same way as a man would act who believed it to be false. There is no third course possible. It is not, then, just to require of the advocate of this doctrine that he should assume an attitude purely apologetic. Nor will the inquirer arrive at practical truth who thinks that he may suspend his decision till every objection has been removed. His task really is to consider and compare two cosmical theories—the one including, and the other excluding the efficacy of prayer, and to decide, upon a review of the whole evidence, which of the two is the more probable.[1]

It is on this principle that I propose to conduct the present inquiry. My object is to present to you, as fully as I can, the evidence on both sides of the question, so as to aid you in determining upon which side the greater probability lies. As in all such cases, a higher probability is all that we can have. It may be a much higher probability, or it may be one which does but just turn the

[1] Appendix, Note B.

Mode of conducting the Controversy. 9

scale; but we must not expect more than a probability. And if we are sometimes disposed to repine, because in matters which so deeply concern our welfare as the truths of religion we cannot have certainty, and are often forced to accept instead a probability which is not high, we must remember that this necessity is in nowise limited to the domain of religion. It is a necessity which meets us everywhere. Nay, it is most imperative, as it seems, most cruel, when the question to be decided is one which may involve the happiness of our whole lives. In trifles —the pursuits of an hour or a day—our path is often clear enough; but in things of the deepest moment, in which a right judgment is to us of the last importance, who has not felt the distracting doubt which tells him how slight is the evidence upon which he is often forced to decide?

The two theories of which I have spoken—that, namely, which includes in the system of the world, and that which excludes from it, the element of prayer—being directly opposed (in technical language, contradictories), and no third theory therefore being possible, it is, logically, immaterial whether we consider successively the arguments in favour of each of these theories respectively, or the arguments against them. I prefer the latter form for the discussion, inasmuch as it is in this form that arguments in favour of the second or prayerless theory are usually presented. These arguments usually appear as objections—objections to the introduction of prayer among the causes which produce or modify phenomena: and the usual mode of conducting the discussion on the other side is to endeavour in the first place to obviate these objections, and then to produce any positive evidence which can be produced on that side. I do not, however, adopt this form of discussion, for the reason already stated, namely, that it allows, at least in appearance, the one disputant to assume an attitude purely sceptical; and as I have before explained to you, we have in the world of practice nothing to do with scepticism. The question really lies between belief and disbelief.

I propose, therefore, to examine successively the arguments against a theory of the world which includes prayer, and the arguments against a theory of the world which excludes prayer. By giving this form to the discussion, neither disputant will be allowed the advantage which belongs to the position of one who assails without being required to defend. Thus the sceptic will be excluded; and the real disputants—the believer and the disbeliever—will be placed, so far as the form of the discussion is concerned, on a footing of perfect equality.

It is necessary in all such inquiries, if we would conduct them fairly, to begin by defining exactly the starting point, if I may so call it. At what stage do we propose to take up the controversy? Do we commence without any assumption, or do we commence at a later stage, assuming the truth of certain principles which we suppose to have been previously established? If we adopt this latter course—and it is that which here we must adopt, if we would confine the discussion within reasonable limits—what are the principles which we assume? An accurate statement of these principles is necessary for two reasons: in the first place, because they are the founda-

Form of Theism assumed.

tion of all the subsequent reasoning; and, secondly, because these principles mark exactly the extent of the conclusions obtained. I need hardly remind you that when we start with an assumption, the conclusion obtained is necessarily conditional—conditional on the truth of the principles assumed. The value of the conclusion therefore depends on the nature of the assumption which has been made.

One principle which necessarily underlies every discussion on the subject of prayer is Theism. Without belief in Theism prayer would be an impossibility, or rather an absurdity. There can be no prayer without belief in the existence of a Being to whom prayer is addressed. Every discussion like the present must, therefore, commence on the one side, with the proof or assumption of the existence of a God.

But a belief in Theism, thus vaguely expressed, is not sufficient to give a standing-ground to the present discussion. There are systems of Theism (so called, at least), under which prayer would be scarcely less absurd than under a system of Atheism. If God be but a name given to the aggregate of the forces of Nature, or to the aggregate of the beneficent forces of Nature—if, in a word, the conception underlying that name be Pantheistic—prayer seems hardly intelligible. In fact, prayer must be addressed to a *person*, not to a force or aggregate of forces. The adoption of the Pantheistic idea would, therefore, stop the whole discussion on the threshold.

I propose, then, to assume the existence of a personal God. I do not enter upon a proof of the truth of this tenet. Such an addition to the present inquiry would lengthen it far beyond its proper limits. Assuming, then, as I propose to do, the truth of this form of Theism, I only remind you, with regard to its proof, that this doctrine belongs to the class already defined. It is one towards which we cannot maintain a sceptical attitude in our lives, whatever we may do in theory. The duties which belief in a Supreme Ruler of the universe brings with it must be either performed or neglected. If you perform them, whatever your speculative belief may be, your life is that of a Theist. If you neglect them, your life is, except perhaps in one particular, that of an Atheist. It is, I know, a favourite position with a certain school of thinkers that, the existence of a God being a question utterly beyond the range of the human intellect, we ought to have no opinion on the subject. But the life of one holding this view does not differ from the life of an Atheist in any respect but one, namely, that an Atheist, holding as he does a definite opinion on the subject, may think himself bound to try to convince others that there is no God; while the Positivist can at most think himself bound to try to convince them that they can never know whether there be or not. But, after all, the practical effect of such a difference is very trifling.

There is another question connected with Theism in its practical relation to man, which, as essential to my present subject, I must here consider. This question may be stated as follows :—Assuming that God does exist, ought we to endeavour to form an idea of His character? and if so, how is this to be done? In other words, are the

Use of Scripture. 13

moral attributes of the Supreme Being a proper subject for man's inquiry?[1] and if so, how is such an inquiry to be conducted, and from what source are we to obtain our information?

Now, in reply to the first question, we may say that some idea of the attributes of God is an essential part of practical Theism. It belongs to that class of questions of which I have more than once spoken. It is a question to which, if we are to remain Theists in any practical sense, we must give *some* answer. To believe in the existence of a God, of whose character we form no conception, is, so far as our lives are concerned, the same as to disbelieve His existence. If Theism is to affect our lives, if the idea of pleasing God is to form one of the motives which prompt our actions, we must have some means of determining, or at least of imagining, what *is* pleasing to Him. In other words, we must form some conception of His character. How is this to be done? With the answer to this question I may fitly conclude this preliminary inquiry.

Some will answer readily enough: "Take your idea from the Bible. There God has revealed as much of His nature as it is fitting that man should know. Accept then reverently that which has been there 'written for your learning.' Question not its truth, how unlike soever it may be to the conclusions at which your unaided reason might have arrived, and seek to know no more."

But it may be fairly urged against this mode of forming a conception of the Divine Nature, that with regard

[1] Appendix, Note C.

to one of the Divine attributes, it is a *petitio principii*. For the highest point to which the evidence for Revelation can attain is to prove that it *is* a Revelation. If this evidence can show that Scripture has come from God, it has done all that it professes to do. But if we would pass from the proof of the origin of Scripture to the proof of its truth, some consideration of the character of God must necessarily intervene. One, at least, of His attributes we must have arrived at before we can thus establish the truth of Revelation. We must believe in the truthfulness of its Author. So far, then, as the attribute of truthfulness is concerned, the character of God cannot be known from Scripture; and it may be fairly contended that any argument in support of the existence of this attribute drawn from Scripture must be fallacious, inasmuch as it begins by assuming that which it professes to prove.

This argument is undoubtedly valid with regard to the one Divine attribute to which it is here applied. We cannot logically build on Scripture our faith in the truthfulness of God, for it is on that very faith that the authority of Scripture rests. But if we can find any other foundation for this belief, we may then avail ourselves of the aid of Scripture to give us information with regard to other Divine attributes. At the same time we shall do well to recollect (and men do not always recollect) that, as no building can be stronger than its foundation, the reliance which we place in the evidence of Scripture ought never to exceed the reliance which we place in the evidence, whatever it may be, which convinces us of the truthfulness of God. What is this evidence?

Original Source of Information.

We must reply by another question. Whence comes our belief in the truthfulness of our own faculties? When our intellect or our moral faculty reveals to us a truth, why do we believe that it *is* a truth, and not a mere figment of our own minds? How do we, who know only the feelings of our minds, come to believe that we have a knowledge of things, not merely as we think them to be, but as they really are? I can conceive but one answer to this question. We believe in our faculties because we cannot help it—because we are impelled to that belief by a force which we can neither evade nor resist; and even when we might seem to surrender our own judgment to that of another, it is upon a faculty of our own that we still rely. We prefer the judgment of another to our own, because our own reason tells us that in this particular case that other is probably better informed than ourselves. If this belief in our own faculties fails, all fails. "There is apparently," says Mr. Goldwin Smith, "no ultimate criterion of truth, either physical or moral, except our inability, constituted as we are, to believe otherwise."[1]

Belief in the truthfulness of our own faculties would seem to lead by necessary consequence to belief in the truthfulness of their author—if they have an author. If man's faculties be the work of God, man can hardly distrust Him without also distrusting them. If He be a deceiver, so, in all probability, are they too. If they are truthful, so too is He. It is thus, I conceive, that

[1] *Macmillan's Magazine*, No. 207, p. 200.

we arrive at belief in the truthfulness of God. As soon as this belief is established, the Bible, if proved to be a revelation, may aid us in acquiring a knowledge of other Divine attributes; *here*, it can give us no assistance, inasmuch as it can have no authority until this belief has been established. While it is right, therefore, in forming our ideas of the other Divine attributes, to avail ourselves of the aid of Revelation, we must remember that the Bible is not the only, nor even the first, source of information on this subject. To disparage the human faculties, as some would do, with the purpose of glorifying the Bible, is to disparage the foundation with the purpose of glorifying the superstructure.

If, then, we would form of the Divine attributes the best conception of which we are capable, we must draw our information from every source which is within our reach—from the Bible certainly—from our own faculties not less certainly—and pre-eminently among them, from the moral faculty. There is no source from which we can more safely derive our information. It is not infallible— what is?—but it is less liable to error than any other human faculty. Even the errors which have been ascribed to it may often be more justly attributed to the intellect. The moral sense may have decided rightly upon the case laid before it, but the case itself was erroneously stated, and this is the fault of the intellect. Thus, for example, it cannot be fairly alleged that the moral sense is incapable of judging of the character of God, *because* it is often incapable, or very imperfectly capable, of deciding what God ought to do in some actual case. The error in the decision of this latter question is most probably not a faulty moral judgment, but an erroneous or imperfect conception of the facts. For this error the intellect, not the moral sense, is justly responsible.

On the whole, then, if we inquire, Ought we to endeavour to form a conception of the character of God? the answer must be—Yes; for without some such conception we cannot be practical Theists. We cannot worship an unknown and unimagined God. And, if we inquire further, Whence is this conception to be derived? the answer must be—Primarily and principally from the moral nature which He has given to man.[1]

I know, indeed, that this source of information is far from being a favourite with some theologians. We have not to search far among schools of theology, before we find presented for man's worship, and even for his love, a portrait of God, which, judged by man's moral nature, is the portrait of a Being unjust, selfish, and cruel. To make the reception of such a portrait possible, it is absolutely necessary to discredit the faculty by which it is condemned, and it is discredited accordingly. But those who reject the testimony of man's moral nature would do well to reflect on all that is involved in that rejection. Discredit *that* testimony, and which of your faculties will you trust? Discredit your faculties, and where will you find a foundation for your religion? But the truth is, that you cannot discredit your faculties in practice, whatever you may do in speculation. Your own faculties are, and must be, the guide of your life. You may fancy that you have surrendered your own judgment to a man, or a

[1] Appendix, Note E.

Church, or a book, but it is upon your own judgment that you still rely—the judgment by which you have recognized the authority of the man, or the Church, or the book. If that judgment be not correct, and it is upon a faculty of your own that you must rely to assure you of its correctness, the whole superstructure of your belief falls to the ground.

If men attempted to carry out consistently the principle of disparaging the human faculties, they would soon be convinced of its logical absurdity. But they are not consistent. Some one favourite faculty is really, though often unconsciously, exempted from the condemnation. And when men believe that they have attained an infallible guide, they are really attributing infallibility to one of their own faculties.

One man thinks that he believes in the infallibility of the true (*i.e.* his own) Church. He is really believing in the infallibility of two judgments of his own mind; one—that the true Church is infallible; the other—that his own is the true Church. Another thinks that he has found an infallible guide in the Bible. But he, too, is attributing infallibility to the human faculty which has ascertained its origin, and to the human faculty which determines its meaning.

I repeat, therefore—Scepticism with regard to the human faculties is universal scepticism. He who created man gave him these faculties for the discovery of truth. If he cannot discover it thus, he cannot discover it at all.

LECTURE II.

THEOLOGICAL ARGUMENTS AGAINST THE EFFICACY OF PRAYER.

ST. MATTHEW, vi. 8.

"Your Father knoweth what things ye have need of, before ye ask him."

HAVING, in my last Lecture, stated the principles on which I propose to conduct the present inquiry, I now proceed to consider the question itself—the question, namely, of the efficacy of Prayer. I have already entered on the statement of this question sufficiently far, to show that it belongs to that practical class which compels a decision. At the risk, however, of some repetition, I wish to state here, at the commencement of the actual investigation, the precise question on which I propose to engage you during the present Course.

Is Prayer a *cause*, in the philosophical sense of that term? Has it real effects? Are there any phenomena which are produced, or modified, by the appearance of Prayer among the antecedents? Or, if this can hardly be disputed (there is, perhaps, no phenomenon which is absolutely inoperative), what is the range of its action? Are its effects altogether restricted to the mind of the individual who prays, or do they extend to the outer world? If they do so extend, is the sphere of the operation of Prayer purely spiritual, or has it power also in the physical world?

I must observe here, that I use the word "prayer," not in that widest signification in which it denotes all communion of the soul with God, but in the narrower sense, in which it comprises only that part of the soul's communion which consists of *petition*—requests addressed by man to God.

Premising this limitation in the use of the word, I proceed to consider our first and greatest question—Has prayer *any* effect besides its reflex action on the soul of him who prays?

Now, it will be conceded on all hands, that prayer can produce an external effect only in one way—namely, by determining the appearance of the Divine volition in the series of antecedents. Prayer is not of the nature of a physical cause. It cannot produce a physical effect by the introduction of a series of purely physical phenomena. It is a petition addressed by man to God, and can act only, like any other petition, by influencing the will of the person to whom the petition is addressed. At the same time, it must be remembered that this action may belong to either of two kinds. It may be either the determining cause which affects the will of the person to whom the petition is addressed, or the condition which that person himself has prescribed, as essential to be fulfilled by any one who wishes for his interference.

Strictly speaking, this latter may also be considered to be a cause; but it is a cause of so peculiar a kind, that it will contribute to clearness if we class it separately. There is another reason for this separate classification, to which I shall allude further on; for the present, I do not enter upon the question between the different theories of the mode of action of prayer, which may be founded on the classification which we adopt. I take up the question simply in this form—Has prayer *any* effect in procuring the interference of the Divine Being? I propose to lay before you, as fully as I can, the evidence and arguments, from whatever source derived, on both sides of this question. I say, *from whatever source derived;* for I must protest against the method, not uncommon in controversy, which makes one *kind* of argument supreme, and then practically refuses to listen to the rest. *Practically* refuses, I say; for although men do not absolutely ignore these arguments, it is often quite plain that they allow to them no share in the decision of the question. That decision is formed in accordance with the favourite *kind* of argument; and the others, if they oppose themselves, are treated as *difficulties*, to be overcome, if possible; or, if that be not possible, frankly admitted to be insurmountable, but, in no case, to be allowed any real weight in deciding the question.

I now proceed to state the arguments against the theory that prayer has a real efficacy, either as a cause or as a condition, in determining the interference of God in the sequence of events. These arguments may be conveniently divided into two classes, which we may denominate, respectively, the theological argument and the philosophic argument.

The first of these arguments is purely Theistic. It is based upon the alleged inconsistency of the theory of prayer with the attributes of God, according to the best conception which we can form of them.

The second argument is wholly independent of Theism; being derived from the alleged inconsistency of this theory with the principle of law, or with the facts which observation has made known to us. I do not mean to say that these two kinds of argument can be kept perfectly distinct. One form of the theological argument does lean a good deal upon considerations which are more nearly scientific than theological. Still the distinction is sufficiently broad to justify its adoption, as a matter of convenient arrangement.

The theological argument against the external efficacy of prayer may be summed up in one phrase—inconsistency with the attributes of God. Shall it be thought, it is urged, that an All-wise Being needs to be informed of that which His creature requires? Does He not already know it far better than the creature can tell Him? And, if we needed anything to complete our assurance upon this point, has not Christ Himself told us, in the words of my text, that "Your Father knoweth what things ye have need of, before ye ask Him"?

Again, and with reference to the same attribute of wisdom— Do you not in prayer ask of God that He will reverse or modify arrangements which we must suppose to be already the best? Have not all the circumstances of the case which has evoked your prayer been already foreseen by Him? If the efficacy of prayer mean anything, does it not mean that prayer has power to change that which God, having fully foreseen all these circumstances, and thus having the whole case before Him, had resolved to do?

Or again, to take another and very favourite form of the argument—Do you not in effect ask God to perform a miracle? That event which you ask Him to hinder or modify is, to the philosophic eye, but one link in an endless chain—one unit in a vast sequence, visible in some small part to us—lost at both sides in the darkness of a real infinity. It may seem a small thing that you ask; but is anything small to which such a relationship attaches? Do you not really ask Him to change at your desire a vast, infinite arrangement, which He has made from all eternity for the sequence of phenomena? Is there, indeed, changeableness in the Most High? And what is man, that such a revolution should be made for him?[1]

Again—and this is the last form of the theological argument on this side of the question which I shall notice—What effect can you attribute to *supplication*—as such? Is God like a weak man, who can be bent from His purpose by mere entreaty? Shall we represent Him as one whose actions are directed, not by reason, but by a mere emotion?

The first of these arguments need not detain us long. Any theory of prayer to which it is applicable must be

[1] Appendix, Note F.

rejected as untrue. If you pray to God under the impression that you are informing him of your wants, you wholly misconceive the proper function of prayer. In fact, such a theory would hardly be consistent with itself. If God does not know our wants, He can hardly know our thoughts, nor therefore our prayers. But the falsity of this theory of prayer, if indeed such a theory be really received by any one, is no argument against prayer itself. Christ Himself, who taught and exhorted His disciples to pray, at the same time warned them against this conception of the nature of prayer: "Your Father knoweth what things ye have need of."

The third of the foregoing arguments (I postpone for the present the consideration of the second) is in every respect more weighty. Any theory of the efficacy of prayer must maintain that God will do for a suppliant something which He will not do for one who does not supplicate. And the question has presented itself to many minds—Do we not thereby attribute to God a weakness? If it be right that the petitioner should have that for which he prays, ought not God to grant it without the petition? and if it be not right, surely He ought not to grant it at all? Does not such a theory represent an All-wise Being as swerving from the right course under the influence of a mere emotion?

Before attempting to estimate the force of this argument, I must remind you, that the efficacy of prayer may be understood in one of two different senses, to one of which only is the present argument strictly applicable. Prayer may either act directly upon the will of God, as it acts upon the will of man, or it may be simply the *condition* which God has prescribed for man's fulfilment before He grants the blessing. It is only to the former of these theories of prayer that the argument is strictly applicable; although an argument somewhat similar may be urged against the other. I shall consider it farther on; at present I proceed to examine the argument which I have already stated.

And, in the first place—Is an emotion a moral defect?[1] If we ask our moral sense to draw for us a character as perfect as possible, will it give in reply a nature from which all emotion is excluded? Is the highest type of humanity, for example, to be found in the man who passes through life owning allegiance to no power but those of reason and conscience—unsympathising with the joys of his fellow-men—untouched by, though not careless of, their sorrows—relieving, but only as a duty, the distress for which he does not feel—giving to misery all he has, but not a tear? Is that our idea of human perfection? And would we, if it were possible, erase or forget the record of tears drawn from the eyes of One greater than man, by the sight of human sorrow or the forecast of human misery? Is that story a blot on the life of Jesus of Nazareth? There can be no doubt as to the answer which these questions would receive. Whatever picture we may draw of *God*, we should regard a *man* wholly devoid of emotion as a mere monster. He is strong, he is upright; we should fear him and admire him; but we should turn from him with repugnance as altogether unlovable. And man's moral nature will never give him

---

[1] Appendix, Note G.

as a perfect ideal a character which cannot command love.

But when we propose to apply the same principle to the ideal of God, we may be met by the answer that such an extension cannot be justified. This is indeed, it may be said, the verdict of our moral nature as regards man. Drawn from man, the picture is a picture only of man. The attempt to find there the lineaments of God is presumptuous and vain. But to this it may, I think, be fairly answered—that this verdict of our moral sense, although derived from man, and primarily applied to man, is one of those which we cannot help regarding as universal in its application. We are compelled by our moral nature to regard the power of commanding love as a moral perfection, and the want of that power as a moral defect, in any being whatsoever: and our moral sense tells us also that love cannot be bestowed on an emotionless being. So far, then, as our moral nature may be trusted (and what may we trust if not that?), it is the absence, and not the presence, of emotion, which is to be regarded as a defect in any being, human or Divine. If this be true, the supposition that some of the Divine actions are prompted by an emotion does not degrade, but exalt, the conception which we have formed of God.

I need hardly remind you that the teaching of Scripture—whatever weight we may assign to that—is altogether coincident with this view. When we are told, that "the Lord pitieth them that fear Him, like as a father pitieth his children"; when Christ tells His disciples, that, because they have loved Him, the Father has loved them; surely it is intended to draw a parallel between the human and the Divine feeling. The one is, confessedly, an emotion : and, if the words used be read according to any ordinary principle of interpretation, they imply that the other is an emotion too. It is, no doubt, sometimes contended, that no more is meant than that the Divine action is such as would, in man, follow from the presence of the emotion; and this interpretation is perhaps barely possible. But it is certainly not the natural interpretation; and if it were really a degradation to our conception of God to attribute emotion to Him, Christ would hardly have used words which were so likely to confirm His disciples in this false conception. I do not, however, dwell on this point, my present argument being based, not on Scripture, but on man's moral sense.

Assuming, then, that the conception of the Divine nature is not degraded by the presence of emotion as an element, we have still to inquire, whether emotion can conceivably be evoked in the Divine mind by human prayer. Is it compatible with the Divine perfections that God should feel compassion—the emotion which prayer would naturally evoke—for one who prays, more strongly than for one who does not pray? What reply does our moral nature make to this question?

Let me put it in a slightly different form. Is it a mere human weakness which prompts man to yield compliance to a suppliant, merely because he is a suppliant? Does our moral nature recognize this tendency, which undoubtedly exists, as deserving of approbation or of censure? It is an undoubted phenomenon of human nature, that the claim which suffering has upon our compassion is enhanced in our eyes, by the fact that the sufferer has implored our assistance. What does our moral sense say to this? Is it a fault or a virtue?

I cannot say that the answer to this question is so positive as in the former case. It is somewhat complicated by the admiration which we certainly feel for uncomplaining sorrow. But what should we say of a man who has no such tendency? What should we say of the parent, if such there be, who feels no desire to grant his child's request, simply because it is his request? I think that we should call him a hard man. I think that we should feel, towards such a character, some portion of the moral repugnance which would be evoked by a character wholly devoid of emotion; and this repugnance is of the nature of moral disapprobation. Doubtless, we should condemn the parent who always yielded to the wish of the child, how unwise and injurious soever such compliance might be. But we should also condemn the parent who felt no desire to yield, and who could refuse his child's earnest petition without some degree of pain. In a word—desire to comply with the child's request is a motive which we expect to find in a parent's heart. It is a motive which is, and ought to be, frequently overcome by other motives; but it ought to be there; and we should regard as morally defective a nature from which it is wholly absent.

Now, if we examine the elements of which prayer to any one consists, or as we should perhaps more correctly say, the feelings of which prayer is the natural result, we shall find no difficulty in understanding the desire to comply with an earnest petition, which exists in every kindly nature. These component feelings, if I may so call them, are two—desire and trust. Prayer is the result of earnest desire for the thing asked for, combined with trust, more or less firm, in the person from whom it is asked, that he will be disposed to grant the request. It is this latter element—often very weak, but never wholly absent—which, I conceive, distinguishes the case of one who prays from the case of one who desires without praying. It is the presence of this element of trust which disposes man to prefer a suppliant to one, quite as deserving perhaps, who does not supplicate. In man, we know as a fact, that there is nothing which more powerfully affects a generous mind than trust reposed in it by another; and, I may add, it is an emotion of which our moral sense entirely approves. Finding its highest expression in the love of the parent for the child, this emotion mingles in all our holiest feelings. It is present, as a powerful element, in love and friendship. The sacred rights of hospitality, as we call them, owe their sacredness to nothing else; and if, among the shades of human guilt, we would distinguish one of surpassing darkness, it is the guilt of trust betrayed. So it is with man.

Now, in reasoning from the case of petition addressed to man to that of petition addressed to God, the principles already laid down allow us to conclude, that the presence of the element of *trust* will justify a preference, on the part of God, for the person in whom that element is present; so that he might fairly receive a blessing, which was withheld from one equally deserving in other respects, from whose mind the element of trust was absent. How entirely this principle pervades the New Testament, I need hardly remind you. In truth, it is the groundwork of Christianity.

Absence of Petitionary Prayer

But it will be said, Does not this principle place another class above those who pray? Is the fullest trust shown by *them*? Or is it not rather shown by the man who, earnestly desiring a blessing, yet forbears to ask for it, because he feels a perfect confidence that, if it be right that he should have it, God will grant it to him? And if He who reads the heart of man find in it that combination, must He not prefer it to the less perfect trust expressed by prayer? Might not even an earthly parent be so entirely trusted, that the requests of the child should have, as their sole object, to inform the parent what things he has need of? And, if he feel the same confidence in his Heavenly Father, who knows all these things before he asks Him, why should he ask at all? A prayerless life may express complete absence of faith; but may not a prayerless life, in this sense of the word prayer, express the very perfection of faith?

Thus stated, and applied to an ideal class, I think that the argument is unanswerable. You will remember that we are now considering the inherent power of prayer to affect (I hope that I do not speak irreverently) the Divine mind. We are not considering the other theory, which represents prayer as a condition for the bestowal of His blessings, which God has Himself imposed; and we therefore, necessarily, leave out of sight all positive command on the subject. Neither do we now discuss the question, whether such a class as that which I have indicated really exists. But if the question be, whether we cannot conceive in man a Theism so exalted as to be, in our present limited sense of the word, prayerless, I think we must reply in the affirmative. The highest development of faith, no less than its non-existence, may conceivably be indicated by a complete absence of petitionary prayer.

To the whole question, then, whether the supposition that the Divine will is affected by prayer be inconsistent with the best conception which we can form of the attributes of God, the reply appears to be, No—it is not inconsistent; although we can conceive a condition of the human mind marked by absence of petitionary prayer, which we might expect to have still more power in affecting the Divine mind. Whether faith so exalted really exists in any human being, is a question which only He to whom all hearts be open can decide.

To complete the examination of the argument which would infer the absolute inefficacy of prayer, irrespectively of the nature of the thing prayed for, from the unchangeable nature of God, it is necessary to consider the other theory, which regards prayer not as a *cause*, in the usual (I can hardly say the proper) sense of the word, but as a *condition*, of which God requires the fulfilment from those who desire to receive a blessing at His hands. It is plain that the argument which we have been examining does not properly apply to this theory. Here there is no direct action on the Divine mind attributed to prayer. It is not then necessary to ascribe to God, as the former theory does, anything of the nature of an emotion. The efficacy of prayer, in this sense, is consistent with the ascription to the Supreme Being of a nature perfectly emotionless. I have given some reasons against the truth of such an ascription; but the conditional theory of prayer does not require the decision of the question in either way. Is there, then, any argument derived from the attributes of

God against the affixing of a condition like this to the grant of the desired blessing?

Directly, as I have said, the argument which we have been considering does not affect this supposition—indirectly, and with diminished force, it does. For it may be contended that, if it be derogatory to the character of God to suppose Him to be moved by man's petition, any practice which tends to encourage that notion is open to serious objection. And it may be contended too, that, whatever men may profess or teach upon this subject, the *practice* of earnest prayer encourages—nay, almost requires—a belief that such prayer does, in the proper sense of the word, influence the Divine will.

The first of these principles is certain; and the second, if not universally true, does, I am sure, faithfully represent the condition of many minds. The argument which we have examined does therefore apply, although indirectly and with diminished force, to the conditional theory of prayer. I say "with diminished force"; for it is one thing to charge a theory with being false, and quite another thing to say that it tends to encourage in some minds, though without teaching it, a serious mistake. Whether or not the notion, that the Divine will can be actually influenced by human prayer, *be* a mistake, is a question which I have already considered. If it be, the first-mentioned theory of prayer is untenable; and a strong, though not absolutely conclusive, objection lies against the other. Not absolutely conclusive—for it is possible, that the advantages, derivable from the existence of such a condition as prayer, might more than counterbalance the injury caused to some minds by the mistake of which I have spoken.

In truth, the objection, that they are productive of some mischief, may be justly alleged against all powerful agents, how good soever their general effect may be. It is a good thing to love our children—to love our country—and yet many a grievous wrong has grown out of the one love, and many a desolating war would have been impossible without the other. It is therefore but in accordance with analogy that such a condition as prayer might be prescribed to man, even if it did tend to develop in some minds an untrue conception of the Divine nature. If the conception so developed be not untrue, the whole argument, as against either theory of prayer, falls to the ground.

Before I pass from this part of my subject, I must add a few words to that which I have already said in justification of the principle of allowing our moral nature to judge of God, as we allow it to judge of man. I have said that we are compelled by a necessity of our nature —that necessity which is our ultimate criterion of truth— to believe that the moral distinctions which our moral sense has made known to us are universal. We cannot believe that the distinction between virtue and vice is due to any peculiarity of our own minds, nor that the moral approval and censure which these qualities call forth from us are applicable only to man. As readily might we believe that the theorems of geometry are figments of the human mind; or that their truth is limited to this earth, and ceases when we pass its bounds, as that time, or place, or person, can obliterate or change the relations which the words virtue and vice, moral approval and moral censure, necessarily present to our minds.

The alternatives then are these—either we must abstain from the attempt to form any conception of the moral attributes of God, or we must judge of those attributes by our own moral nature. The adoption of the former alternative would give to man a life differing in no important respect from that of an Atheist. We might raise altars to "The unknown God"; but there our worship would necessarily end. I cannot see how any sentiment, other than a vague feeling of awe, could be excited by a Being of whose nature we had formed no conception. If, on the other hand, we do attempt to form such a conception, the moral qualities which we attribute to God must be similar in kind to those of which our moral nature approves in man. Thus, when we speak of the justice or the mercy of God, our words, if they have any meaning, must denote qualities similar to those which we call by the same names when we find them in men. In either case, the word denotes a quality which evokes in our minds a particular kind of moral approbation; and, by a necessity of our nature, this approbation is universally evoked by the same quality, in whatever being it may be present. Thus, I conceive, we are justified by the necessities of practical Theism in attempting to form *a* conception of the moral attributes of God: and we are justified by the felt universality of moral distinctions in forming that conception by the aid of our moral nature.

I should now proceed to consider an argument which is perhaps more frequently heard than any other theological argument on this side of the controversy, and which is conveyed in the question, Do we not ask God to work a miracle on our behalf, at least in all the cases in which the benefit asked for is physical? Do we not ask Him to reverse or modify the order of nature for our pleasure? And is not such a request utterly unreasonable, disrespectful to the Supreme Ruler of the Universe, and based upon a total misconception of His character, and of the relation which subsists between us and Him?

But this argument is too important to be examined shortly. Capable as it is of brief and simple statement, it will be found to involve principles and to open out questions requiring to be considered at some length; and I must therefore postpone the examination of it till my next Lecture.

LECTURE III.

THEOLOGICAL ARGUMENTS AGAINST THE EFFICACY OF PRAYER—MIRACLES.

St. Matthew, x. 29.

"Are not two sparrows sold for a farthing? and one of them shall not fall on the ground without your Father."

IN my last Lecture I concluded, as you may remember, the examination of an argument which would infer the inefficacy of petitionary prayer in general from the best conception which we can form of the attributes of God. This argument is wholly independent of the particular object of the petition itself, and is equally applicable, whether the thing asked for belong to the world of spirit or to the world of matter.

The argument which I have now to examine professes to have a more limited scope. Those who make use of it do not usually deny the efficacy of prayer in all cases. Leaving it untouched when its object is a spiritual blessing, they only seek to exclude the physical world from its operation. They will allow man to ask that his faith may be strengthened, or that his heart may be purified;

but they deny the propriety of prayer for temporal blessings. Against such prayer they direct the argument which we have now to consider; and it would seem that they limit the argument to prayer having this purpose. I need hardly, however, remind any logician that the limits of an argument do not depend upon the will of him who uses it. It may suit his purpose to apply it only to a particular case, and even, in other cases, to take up a position inconsistent with it; but the limits of an argument depend upon the argument itself, and not upon the application which the controversialist may choose to make of it. It is then, in dealing with any such argument, important to inquire, What is its legitimate scope? Does ✓ the restricted use made of it denote a real limitation, or is it merely arbitrary? We shall find this inquiry to be in the present case of much importance.

When it is proposed to pray to God for any physical benefit, as, for example, for the arrest of a famine or a pestilence, it is often objected—Are you not asking Him to perform a miracle? That physical phenomenon which you ask Him to remove or to reverse is the result of a train of physical causes reaching back to the commencement of all things, if they had a commencement—infinite, if they had not. Is it credible—would it be right—that God should break this chain to gratify you? Are not miracles (and you ask for no less), if they have ever existed, to be regarded as rare exceptions to the orderly course of nature? Do you expect to change them into matters of every-day occurrence? And when you ask of God thus to interfere, ✓ are you not in effect regarding Him as an unskilful mechanician, whose work is so imperfect as to require this constant meddling? Is not such a petition necessarily useless? Worse than that, is it not dishonouring to God, so far as you can dishonour Him?

I have said that this argument is commonly directed only against prayer for physical results; and I now proceed to inquire, in the first place, whether this limitation be justifiable. It is said that, in praying for the production of a physical effect, we ask God to perform a miracle. Is this true? and if it be true, is it true of such prayer only?

I am obliged to touch here on the well-worn question of miracles; and it is with special reference to this part of my subject, that I have spoken of the difficulty of keeping perfectly distinct the theological and the philosophic arguments against prayer. For the uniformity of nature and the attributes of the Author of nature are so closely connected, that it is impossible to preserve a perfectly sharp distinction between considerations drawn from these conceptions respectively. But the argument itself is in nowise affected by this slight want of precision, which is indeed more apparent than real.

Is it then true that in asking for a physical benefit we ask for a miracle, while in asking for a spiritual benefit we do not? What is a miracle?[1]

It is, some will say, a violation, or a suspension (these words really mean the same thing) of the laws of nature. It is, others will tell us, a display of superhuman power— the performance, by the power of God, of something which is beyond the power of man. I shall endeavour to show,

---

[1] Appendix, Note H.

further on, that the former definition is inaccurate. The second is true, but with this reservation, that in order to constitute a miracle it is not necessary that the result itself should be beyond the power of man. The restoration of sight to the blind man would not lose its miraculous character, if it could be shown that the case was not beyond the power of a skilful oculist. But if we take into account both the result and the physical means employed, the transaction *was* a display of superhuman power, and the definition is fully justified. Let me explain this to you a little more at length.

We know that man's will, without the intervention of man's body, has no power on anything external to himself. A mental antecedent may have its immediate consequent in the mind or body of the individual, and, so far as we know, only there. If an antecedent in the mind of an individual have a remote consequent without him, we know that some phenomenon in the *body* of the individual must have intervened in the series. And this is equally true, whether the remote consequent be itself physical or mental. You cannot cause a pebble to rise from the ground, however earnestly you may desire it, without the intervention of your body. You cannot affect the mind of your fellow-man, however strongly you may will it, without the intervention of your body. Thoughts the most burning, until they are clothed in words, or find some other bodily expression, have no power beyond the individual in whose heart they are formed. So it is with the work of man.

But it is otherwise with the work of God. There a mental antecedent *is* followed by an immediate external consequent. This consequent may not indeed be itself the end of the Divine action. Between the mental purpose and the final result may intervene, as in the actions of man, any number of links; but the essential difference between the actions of God and the actions of man is this —that in the former case there is an immediate transition from a volition to an external result.

And this, I conceive, is also the essential difference of a miracle. It is not merely that the result is wonderful. There is no one of these results which we might not conceive to be effected by means to which, however they might astonish us, we should never think of giving the name "miraculous." Take the most wonderful of all— the raising of a dead body to life. We know that galvanism has succeeded in reproducing some of the vital phenomena. Suppose the discovery to be announced of a yet more powerful agent which should reproduce *all* these phenomena—an agent which should restore all the vital powers, not for a moment but permanently; so that these powers should continue to act when the work of the restoring agent had ceased. We should receive such an announcement with immense scepticism. We should require for the proof of its truth the most overpowering evidence. If convinced of its reality, we should call it wonderful in the extreme; but we should not call it miraculous. We should say—It is the result of a physical combination hitherto untried. It is new. It is unlike anything which has been done before; it is utterly marvellous; but it is not a miracle. But if it be true that Lazarus rose from his tomb at the command of Christ, then we do call that result a miracle. Why? Because, the physical antece-

Essential Difference of a Miracle. 41

dents being obviously inadequate to the production of such a consequent, we are forced to attribute it to an immediate mental antecedent—a mental cause which is capable of producing an immediate external effect. It is this which convinces us of the presence of superhuman power. It is this which constitutes a miracle. And I do not hesitate to say that, if the time should ever come when man can produce by his simple volition an immediate external result, the generic difference between miracles and ordinary phenomena will have disappeared.

We are now in a position to consider whether the distinction which, while excluding prayer from the physical world, would leave the spiritual world still open to it, be founded on reason.[1] The exclusion of the operation of prayer from the physical world is, so far as this argument is concerned, based on the idea that, in asking God to grant us a physical benefit, we ask Him to perform a miracle. But we have seen, I think, that this is equally true if the benefit asked for be spiritual. There, as here, we ask for the exertion of a power transcending, not only in degree but in kind, the power of man. There, as here, we ask for an action possessing the distinctive character of a miracle, namely, a volition followed by an immediate external result. The truth is that, to ask God to act at all and to ask Him to perform a miracle, are one and the same thing.

There are certain causes which tend to conceal this truth from our minds. For example, there is a very common saying that "God works by means." Now, if it

[1] Appendix, Note I.

be meant by this saying that between the Divine volition and the final result a long series of physical causes is frequently interposed, the saying is quite true. If it be meant that, at some remote period, God established a cause or system of causes, by the sole action of which, and without further action on His part, all phenomena are now produced, such a supposition would amount to a denial of any direct action on God's part, and would therefore banish petitionary prayer altogether. This, however, is, quite plainly, not the sense in which the saying is used. But if it be meant that the action of God is *ever* strictly analogous to the action of man, then the saying is not true. Whatever be the length of the interposed physical series, there is one link which takes it out of the category of human actions—a volition followed by an immediate external result.

But the principal cause which leads men to admit readily, and without calling it miraculous, the direct action of God on the human mind, while they at once give that name to any direct action of God on the human body, is, I suppose, the obscurity which surrounds mental, as compared with physical, sequences. We cannot indeed, except in some few cases, assign with accuracy to a physical phenomenon its system of antecedents, or, as we call it, its cause. Still we are not wholly in the dark, and can generally form some rough idea on the subject. But how often are we wholly in the dark as to the cause of a mental phenomenon? Of the sequences in other minds we know almost nothing. But even in each man's own mind, how often do thoughts spring up so completely "unbidden," to use a common phrase, that

Limitation of Argument not justified. 43

he can form no idea whatever of their cause? And so he accepts without difficulty the theory of a direct spiritual influence, not as exceptional, but as an ordinary occurrence. But I must remind you that the question is not whether the occurrence be usual or unusual, but whether it bear impressed upon it the character of a miracle. And, if by a miracle be meant the exertion of a power transcending, not only in degree but in kind, the power of man, that name attaches to the intervention of God in the spiritual world no less than to His intervention in the physical world. If then it be an objection to prayer for temporal blessings, that we therein ask God to perform a miracle, it is equally an objection to prayer for spiritual blessings. You ask Him to perform as real a miracle, when you ask Him to cure your soul of a sin, as you do when you ask Him to cure your body of a fever. The other meaning attached to the word miracle, in which it is supposed to involve a violation of the principle of law, I shall consider more appropriately when I come to examine the philosophic objections to the doctrine of prayer.

Hitherto my object has been to show you, that the scope of the argument which we have been examining is more extended than is supposed by many of those who use it, and that if we are to allow it the power of excluding prayer from the world of matter, we must allow it also the power of excluding prayer from the world of spirit. We have now to consider a more important question. Is the argument itself valid? Is it in truth derogatory to the character of God that we should ask, or expect Him to interfere? I take, as the case most favourable to those who advance the argument, the application which they themselves make. Let the question then be—Is it derogatory to the attributes of God to suppose that He interferes in the world of matter—to supply a dearth, or to arrest a pestilence? To this question many answer: Yes, it is derogatory to His attributes. For by making such a supposition you in effect assign to Him (to use again a favourite analogy) the character of an unskilful mechanician, whose work will not fulfil its purpose without constant interference on the part of the maker.

Now it *is* derogatory to the character of the mechanician that his work should require this constant interference. For his purposes are capable of being fully carried out by mechanism; nay, the very machine which he has made professes to carry them out, and is rightly considered imperfect if it do not. But, before we accept the application of this analogy to the works of God, we must ask—Is it derogatory to His character to suppose that He has purposes which cannot be effected by any system of mechanism, however perfect? Is it derogatory to His character to suppose that He has powers, and uses them in the government of the universe, which cannot be transferred to any system of mere matter, however admirable its arrangement might be?

How should we decide a similar question in the case of man? Suppose that it were suddenly revealed to us, that the machine of the thirtieth century would have as much power as the man of the nineteenth. Suppose that we could foresee that our successors of the thirtieth century would be able to construct a machine capable of doing, unaided, all that we of the nineteenth can do by any means. I suppose we should say that such an achievement indicated an enormous development of the human intellect. But suppose that we were told further, that this machine would do, not only all that we of the nineteenth century can do, but all that the men of the thirtieth century themselves could do, and even all that they wished to do. I think that we should call this a very one-sided development of the human intellect; for it would imply that, while the machine-producing power of the human mind had advanced with prodigious rapidity, its other powers and—more than that—its aims, had, comparatively, stood still. It is, we generally think, but a poor spirit whose aims do not soar far above its powers. But what should we say of one whose aims rose no higher than the power of a machine which he himself could make? If we wished to draw an ideal picture of intellectual perfection, should we do so by effacing that superiority of mind which has hitherto rendered so many of its powers intransferable to matter? Shall we regard the possession of these intransferable powers as being itself a mark of imperfection? Is the superiority of mind over matter indeed but temporary, and do we look for a day when it shall have passed away for ever? Nay, my brethren, there is that in the human mind which tells quite another story. There is that in the human mind which bids us look into the future, with the anticipation, not that the powers of mind and of matter will ever be equalized, but rather that the inherent superiority of the former will every day become more marked.

For, what is human life? Is it not one long battle

between the spirit of man and those powers of organized matter which we call the forces of nature? And who does not know the history of that battle—a battle often lost, but always renewed, and with ever-increasing success —the history of one combatant often defeated, but always advancing—of another, often victorious, but always driven back? And if the spirit of man can smile now at material dangers before which it once sunk helpless and hopeless, does that point to a time when the powers of mind and matter shall be equalized? Is not the story of that battle a proof, if there were no other, of an inherent superiority?

There is yet another point. If there be in the powers of the human spirit a continued advance which matter does not share, is not this even more strikingly true of its aspirations? Does not each one of us feel that, how rapid soever may be the advance of his actual powers, his aspirations advance more rapidly still? Do not the philosopher and the savage differ even more in their aspirations than they differ in their actual powers?[1]

Now, my brethren, would you call it a mark of imperfection in the human spirit that it should never be able to efface the signs of its own superiority—that it should never be able to construct a machine which should replace itself? Is it derogatory to man, that the powers of his intellect should keep ever in advance of the powers of any system of matter, however admirably he may himself have arranged it? Nay, is it not rather his glory? And if it be, shall we call it derogatory to the Infinite

[1] Appendix, Note K.

Divine Purposes cannot be effected by Mechanism. 47

Spirit, that the marks of His ineffable superiority are ineffaceable even by Him? Is it unworthy of Him, that even He cannot construct a machine which could replace Himself—that He should have purposes which no system of matter could fulfil? Surely not.

Before, therefore, we are justified in rejecting, as derogatory to the character of God, the theory that He does interfere in physical sequences, we ought to have evidence to convince us that it is at least improbable that He has any purposes which cannot be fulfilled by a machine. Thus, if we were asked, Is it not a clumsy and circuitous way of producing a physical effect, to arrange a system of antecedents which would produce a different effect, and then to modify their natural result by direct interference, when the physical antecedents might have been so arranged as to produce the required effect without interference? the answer is, Yes, if no more was intended than the production of the physical effect. Thus, for example, when the advocate of the efficacy of prayer contends that a pestilence may have been arrested by the interference of God, he may be asked, Might not the same effect have been produced in a manner more simple, and therefore more consistent with the Divine perfections, by so arranging the physical antecedents that the pestilence should only last the required time? The answer is, Yes, if no more were intended than that the pestilence should last for a certain time. But before you ask me to reject the "dogma of interference" as inconsistent with the attributes of God, you are bound to produce evidence sufficient to make it at least probable that among the Divine purposes there were none which might not have been fulfilled by a purely physical sequence. Can any such evidence be produced?

It is certainly not true that the antecedents to a purely physical event are in all cases themselves purely physical. On the contrary, the voluntary actions of men occupy, as we know, a large part of these sequences. Whatever may be said of the dogma of Divine interference, the dogma of human interference is undoubted. There are few physical sequences wholly free from it: and yet this method of producing an effect is quite as circuitous, and, if Divinely appointed, quite as inconsistent with the attributes of God, as the Divine interference is supposed to be. Thus, in the case already referred to, let it be supposed that the physical causes, acting by themselves, would produce a pestilence lasting for a year. But the interference of man devises a remedy which puts an end to the pestilence in six months. If we regard this arrangement as being of Divine appointment, may we not ask why this circuitous method was resorted to, and why the purely physical antecedents were not originally so arranged that the pestilence should only last for six months? But there is an obvious answer:—Because the arrest of the disease by the voluntary action of man fulfils purposes—certainly with regard to himself, probably with regard to the physical world also—which could not have been effected by a purely physical sequence. Is it unreasonable to apply the same principle to Divine interference? May not similar purposes exist there also? If it be the Divine appointment that the spirit of man should intervene in physical sequences, is it improbable that the Spirit of God should do the same? Certainly the argument from analogy

Inconsistent Objection to Divine Interference. 49

seems to point the other way. What the purposes effected by the Divine interference may be supposed to be, or whether we have any means of forming an idea on the subject, are questions which I hope to consider at a later stage of the present inquiry.

I have thus endeavoured to lay before you, so far as I know them, that class of arguments directed against the efficacy of prayer which I have called theological, as being deduced from conceptions of the attributes of God. I cannot say that they appear to me to possess any great weight. The first is deduced mainly from the Stoic ideal of mental perfection. I believe this ideal, as applied to either God or man, to be wholly untrue; and I am sure that if we could see it realised in man, our moral nature would turn from it with repugnance. To give weight to the second objection, it is necessary to form a conception of the purposes of God with regard to the universe, which seems to me to be a very limited one; and to produce evidence sufficient to show that this conception is probable. I do not think that such evidence can be produced; nay, as I have endeavoured to show, the argument from analogy appears to point to an opposite conclusion.

Before leaving this part of my subject, I wish to point out an inconsistency (at least it so appears to me) in the theory which would exclude the interference of God from physical, while admitting it in mental sequences. The truth is, that this theory really admits the very kind of interference to which it objects. That man interferes in physical sequences is certain. If, then, God interferes in the sequences of human thought, He interferes in physical sequences, not directly, but quite as effectually as if He acted on the physical phenomena themselves. If it be derogatory to the character of God to assume that He interferes in physical sequences *directly*, it is quite as derogatory to His character to assume that He interferes *indirectly*. Thus the interference of God with the sequence of physical causes which produces a pestilence is equally real, whether He act directly on the causes themselves, or suggest a remedy to the mind of a physician; and, if we cannot assume the one kind of interference without representing Him as an unskilful mechanician who is obliged to mend his own work, neither can we assume the other without a like imputation.

In my next Lecture I hope to conclude the inquiry into the evidence against a system of the world which includes prayer, by examining that class of arguments which I have called philosophic, and which are based on a supposed inconsistency of this system with the principle of Law, or with the facts which observation has made known to us. I have only to add, in concluding the examination of the theological arguments on the same side of the question, that the ideal on which they are based is certainly not a popular ideal. The history of man tells us, that his moral nature does not willingly draw for itself the picture of a God who refuses to listen to prayer. But I hope to speak more fully of this hereafter.

LECTURE IV.

PHILOSOPHIC OBJECTIONS TO THE EFFICACY OF PRAYER.

St. Matthew, x. 29.

"Are not two sparrows sold for a farthing? and one of them shall not fall on the ground without your Father."

HAVING, in my last Lecture, concluded the examination of the arguments against the efficacy of prayer which I have called theological, I now proceed to examine, in accordance with our original division, the more purely philosophic arguments on the same side of the question. These arguments, differing from each other in their nature, and, as I think we shall see, in their weight, agree in this, that they are in no sense Theistic. They make no assumption with regard to the attributes of God, nor even with regard to His existence. Leaving such questions wholly aside, these arguments deal with the theory of the efficacy of prayer as they would deal with any other physical theory; proposing to show, either that the theory itself is *à priori* improbable, as being apparently inconsistent with some established principle; or that it is unreal, because the results which it predicts are inconsistent with facts.

In examining these arguments we must be careful to guard against two opposite errors into which some have fallen. We may, as some have done, declare the ordinary methods of physical science to be inapplicable to the present case. This position is wholly untenable. The theory of prayer asserts that many of its results are physical phenomena; and all physical phenomena are amenable to the methods of physical science. It must be remembered, however, that if these methods are so applied as to violate the conditions imposed by the theory, the result of such an investigation, considered as affecting the truth of the theory, is not reliable. We shall find the importance of this reservation further on.

But there is an opposite error into which we may also fall, namely, decision of the question by physical considerations only, all other arguments being set aside. This exclusive mode of deciding questions, popular as it is, cannot be justified unless the argument to which this exclusive privilege is given has the force of demonstration. If it can only furnish *probable* results, it is plain that these may be outweighed by the opposing probabilities of the arguments which we have neglected. Now, in the present case, if it could be absolutely proved that the theory of the efficacy of prayer is inconsistent with a thoroughly established principle, or with observed facts, we should be justified in rejecting it without further inquiry. But if neither inconsistency can be absolutely proved, the argument derived from its probability, if it be probable, can only take its place among other argu-

Principle of Law. 53

ments, without any exclusive right to decide the question.

It is said—and this is, perhaps, the most popular argument against the efficacy of prayer—that this theory is contrary to the principle of Law. If this proposition, understood in the proper sense of the words, were established, it would go far to render any further discussion unnecessary. But I do not think that it is always understood in the proper sense of the words, and I shall have occasion to point out an improper sense in which it seems to have been used, and in which it is very much less forcible. For the present I take the words in their proper sense; and I proceed to inquire, whether it be true, that the theory of the efficacy of prayer is contrary to the general principle of Law.

What *is* the general principle of Law? Taken in the strictest sense of the word, the principle of Law is this—that the same system of antecedents will always, √ and everywhere, be followed by the same consequent. Expressed in more popular language, it declares, that the same cause is always and everywhere followed by the same effect. The change of time or place, if it leave the antecedents unchanged, leaves the consequent unchanged also. This is the principle of Law in its strictest sense. Now, to render justifiable the application of this principle to any particular case, it must be ascertained that the *entire* system of antecedents, and not the physical antecedents only, are identical in the cases which are compared with each other. Thus it is no violation of the principle of Law to assert, that the introduction of a volition into one of two identical conditions of the human body determines a totally different result. There is a movement in the one case; there is none in the other; but the principle of Law remains inviolate.

So, too, it is no violation of the principle of Law, to suppose that the introduction of a Divine volition into one of two identical systems of antecedents should determine a wholly different consequent; and it is this, and nothing else, which is asserted by the doctrine of the efficacy of prayer. It is not asserted that, as a result of prayer, a different consequent follows from the same system of antecedents; but it *is* asserted, that, as a result of prayer, a new antecedent appears, and that thus the consequent is changed. Whether this really be so is another question, but it certainly *may* be so without any violation of the principle of Law.

This argument against the efficacy of prayer takes sometimes a different form of expression. He who prays is said to ask for a violation, not of the general principle of Law, but of some one or more of the actual laws of Nature. And if it be true, as I think it is, that prayer asks for a miracle, this form of the argument derives support from a very common definition of a miracle, namely, that it is a violation, or (to borrow the usual euphemism) a suspension, of some law of Nature. It is then important to inquire whether this definition be correct.

I have called this argument a different form of expression of the former argument; and this is true, for the second, so far as it is valid, is identical with the first. If the law of Nature, which is said to be violated (or suspended), be a real law, it cannot be violated without a violation of the principle of Law itself. The inviolability of any particular law of Nature is connected with the inviolability of the principle of Law, as the truth of any one of a number of particular propositions is connected with the truth of the universal which contains them all. If the principle of Law be true, and if any asserted law of Nature can be shown to have been violated in a single instance, the alleged law is untrue. To say, then, of a miracle that it is a violation of *a* law of Nature, and to say that it is a violation of *the* principle of Law, are one and the same thing. It must be remembered, however, that any one who employs this argument in its second form is bound to show, not only that the asserted law has been violated, but also that the asserted law is really a law. Without such proof the argument is obviously invalid; and I think that asserted violations of the principle of Law will be often found to mean no more than violations of something which the objector assumes to be a law. It is in this assumption that the weakness of the argument commonly lies.

Is a miracle a violation (or suspension) of any law of Nature? Take for example any one of the miracles of Christ. What law of Nature was violated by the raising of Lazarus, if such a thing really happened? That it is impossible to restore life to a dead body? No such negative law exists, or could exist. All that we are justified in saying is this, that this result cannot be effected by any combination which man has hitherto tried. That no mere word could effect such a result? This is true; but it is not supposed that the result was effected by a mere word. The nearest approach to a law of Nature which was violated by the supposed miracle is that to which I have already alluded, namely, that a volition cannot be followed by an immediate result external to the individual who wills. Now, it is always a matter of uncertainty to establish a negative law: still, notwithstanding some asserted phenomena, it does seem to be a natural law that man's will, without the intervention of man's body, is powerless upon the external world. But we have no right to extend this law to the Divine volitions; nor indeed could we do so, consistently with any system of Theism which ascribes action at any time to the Divine Being. If a Divine volition cannot be followed by an external consequent, it is hard to see how the Deity, unless corporeal, can act at all, or could have acted at any time. Only an Epicurean theology would be possible under such a limitation.

I might now pass on from this argument; but the idea that a miracle implies a suspension of Law, or of some particular law, is so widely spread among persons of all theological opinions, that it may be well to say a few words more for the purpose of showing its falsity.

Take the following example :—Walking along a dangerous path, you slip, and are about to fall over a cliff. You call to a friend who is near to save you. Do you ask him to suspend the law of gravity? Certainly not. You ask him to overcome the *force* of gravity by opposing to it the stronger force of the muscles of his arm; and whether he comply with your request or not, the law of gravity continues equally in force. This we all know.

Now suppose that, instead of calling on a human

No Law of Nature violated by Miracle. 57

friend, you call on God to save you. Experience has indeed taught us that God does not usually grant such requests. But our present question is not whether the request is likely to be granted, but what the request itself implies. Do you, in that request, ask of God that He will suspend the law of gravity? No more than if you addressed the same prayer to a man. Here, as there, you ask that the *force* of gravity may be overcome by a stronger force. The difference between the two cases is this, that the exertion of the Divine volition has an immediate effect upon the external world, which a human volition has not; and that there may be, although we cannot certainly say that there is, in the Divine action an actual creation of force in its material sense, which certainly does not accompany the human action. You do not, then, when you pray for a physical benefit, ask for the suspension of any law of Nature, unless there be a law of Nature which negatives the direct action of the Divine will. If there be such a law, the Divine Being must be, and must have been in all time, absolutely inactive. Even the creation of protoplasm or of a fire-mist must be declared to be impossible. Such a supposition could lead to no conclusion but Atheism (as distinguished from Antitheism). For it would be impossible to adduce any evidence of the existence of a Being who is devoid of all power of external action.

To sum up, then, in a few words, that which has been said on this branch of the subject. When you ask God to do anything—when you ask Him to produce any effect, physical or moral, you ask for a miracle. You ask for the exertion of a power differing in kind from any power possessed by man; and the object of your prayer is no less *a miracle*, when you ask God to act upon your mind, than when you ask Him to act upon your body. But you do *not* ask for the suspension of any law of Nature; unless there be a law which would deprive the Deity of all power, and thus reduce Him to practical non-existence, for the past no less than for the future.

The Philosophic argument against the efficacy of prayer which I now proceed to consider is in every respect different from those which we have been examining—different in kind—different also in weight. It does not accuse the doctrine against which it is directed of inconsistency with any principle, Theistic or philosophic. It simply says—the efficacy of prayer in the physical world is not a fact. And it proposes to establish the truth of this assertion by the ordinary methods of physical inquiry—observation and experiment. You believe, it says to the advocate of prayer, that certain physical results are thereby produced. *How* they are produced is a question with which we have no concern, nor do we take any exception to your theory on that score. But many of the asserted results of prayer are ordinary physical phenomena, whose existence, if they be real, ought to show itself to the ordinary modes of physical inquiry; and if this inquiry fail to detect the existence of such a cause, we must refuse to acknowledge its reality. It is not merely that this reality is *unproved* by physical methods. We believe that we can subject the series of phenomena, in which prayer is supposed to intervene, to physical tests, which must show the reality of this cause, if it be real; and as these tests give no indication of its existence, we must believe it to be not merely unproved but untrue.

I now proceed to consider this argument in detail; but before doing so, I may remark, that it is not to be met by any general declarations of the inapplicability of physical methods of inquiry to such a problem as this. The disputant who denies or limits the applicability of physical methods to the investigation of alleged physical facts, whatever be the supposed cause, is bound to show the reason for this denial or limitation. If he cannot show this, the general principle holds good, namely, that the methods of inductive science are applicable to all physical phenòmena.

The physical method of investigation applied, in the argument which I have now to consider, to the doctrine of the efficacy of prayer, is that which is technically known as "the method of differences." It is proposed to take two series of antecedents, differing only in this, that prayer enters into the one series, and not into the other, and then to determine by observation whether there be any corresponding difference between the consequents. If there be, we are bound to admit the efficacy of prayer; if there be not, we are equally bound to deny it. It is admitted that in this, as indeed in nearly all cases, the application of the method of differences is attended by one serious difficulty, namely, that we do not readily find two series of antecedents, or in common language two cases, which differ only in the presence or absence of prayer. It is proposed to overcome this difficulty in one of the following ways, both which are in common use among physicists.

Argument from Experiment.

The first is the method of experiment. The use of this method enables us, it is thought, to obtain by actual combination two series of antecedents differing only in the one element. This is the principle of the celebrated "hospital test." It was proposed, as many of you know, to take two wards of the same hospital, to each of which the same class of patients should be sent, great care being taken, in the allotment of the patients, to give to neither ward any advantage over the other. Then it was proposed to invite the Christian world, or a part of it, to pray for the recovery of the patients in one ward, leaving those in the other ward unprayed for; and finally, after the process had been continued long enough to form a sufficient induction, it was proposed to examine the respective percentages of recovery, for the purpose of determining whether the ward for which prayer had been made could show a more favourable return. If so, the efficacy of prayer would be established; if not, it is contended that the principle of the method of differences requires us to reject the doctrine as untrue.

This experiment was, I presume, never actually tried: indeed, for reasons upon which I need not now enter, it would be very difficult to make it. But let us suppose that the experiment was made, and with this result, that no difference between the respective percentages of recovery could be detected. What does the principle of the method of differences require us to infer from this? The general inefficacy of prayer? Certainly not; but the inefficacy of prayer *under the conditions of the experiment*. I need not tell any physicist that we cannot deny the existence of a force merely

Legitimate Inference from this Argument. 61

because under certain conditions its effect is not perceptible.

Now, if prayer were an ordinary physical force, its effect would be, of course, independent of the motives of the person employing it. These motives are not, in such a case, to be reckoned among the essential conditions of the phenomenon, nor can their variation in anywise change the effect. But it is not so with prayer. Prayer, if it produce any effect, produces it by acting on the will of a sentient Being, who knows perfectly the motives by which the petitioner is actuated. Analogy, if we had no other reason, would lead us to infer, that the nature of these motives is an important element in determining the success or failure of such action. The motive of the petitioner being thus an essential part of the phenomenon which we have to study, it is plain that we should not be justified in arguing from the case of prayer presented with one kind of motive to that of prayer presented with a kind of motive wholly different. Assuming, therefore, that the experiment was tried; and that the result was to establish a perfectly uniform percentage of recovery, as between the two wards, the legitimate inference would be this, and no more—that prayer, *tried as an experiment*, will not succeed. If there be any theory which predicts the success of experimental prayer, the result of the experiment, if such were the result, would be fatal to it. But I am not aware that there is any such theory. Certainly it is not the Christian theory. The teaching of Christ with regard to the conditions necessary to successful prayer is quite different. He does not say—Try the experiment fairly, and you will succeed; but, "What things soever ye desire, when ye pray, believe that ye receive them, and ye shall have them."[1] "If thou canst believe, all things are possible to him that believeth."[2] Christ teaches us, in fact, that trust in the goodness of God should precede prayer, not follow it.

It has been said to be derogatory to the character of God to suppose that prayer could be rendered ineffectual by the presence of such a motive. I shall examine this argument further on. At the present stage of the discussion such an examination would be out of place, as it would lead us back into the region of Theism, with which I have here no concern. My present purpose is only to determine the legitimate inference to be drawn from the assumed result of a certain experiment. And, I repeat, this inference is, not the inefficacy of prayer in general, but the inefficacy of prayer when offered as an experiment. The proposed experiment, therefore, appears to me to be devoid of weight, as directed against the Christian theory of prayer; and any other experiment having the same purpose would be open to the same objection.

I come now to consider a philosophic argument, agreeing with the last, in that it is based on the method of differences, but differing from it, in that it employs observation, not experiment, to obtain its facts, and is therefore not open to the objection which we have seen to lie against the other. To speak technically, the former argument seems to me to be an *ignoratio elenchi;* the present argument certainly is not.

[1] St. Mark, xi. 24.   [2] St. Mark, ix. 23.

Argument from Statistics—Example. 63

This argument may be stated generally as follows:—

There are certain classes of phenomena, into whose antecedents prayer enters more largely than it does into the antecedents of other phenomena of a similar kind. Hence it is inferred that, if prayer be really efficacious, its efficacy ought to be shown by a corresponding difference in the results. We have, therefore, only to examine the statistics of such phenomena, and if no marked difference can be detected, we are justified in denying the efficacy of prayer, at least in phenomena of that kind.

Thus, for example, if we would know whether prayers for longevity have any real effect, we have only to examine the vital statistics of a class in whose behalf this prayer is more frequently offered than in the case of ordinary men. Such a class we have in reigning Sovereigns. "Grant the King a long life" is quite a common prayer. If, then, statistical tables show no superiority in length of life to be enjoyed by Kings, may we not infer that, in their case at least, prayer is inefficacious? And if it be without effect in their case, does not analogy lead us to infer that prayer for long life is without effect in any case? If this be so, is there not a general presumption against the efficacy of prayer for any physical benefit? It is plain, too, that this presumption is strengthened by every additional case of the same kind.

It has been attempted to turn away the force of this reasoning by general assertions that the statistical method ought not to be applied to questions like the present. But for such assertions I can see no ground. The method of differences, and statistics as its proper auxiliary, are applicable to every case in which an asserted cause and an asserted effect are both within the cognizance of man. This condition is fulfilled in the present case. The effect, namely, the longevity of a certain class, is altogether within human cognizance; and although the same cannot be said of each individual unit in the complex cause—for we cannot look into each man's heart and decide whether his prayer be real or merely formal—yet we are justified in assuming that, among so great a number of prayers, many are genuine. The use, therefore, which this argument proposes to make of statistics and of the method of differences appears to me to be quite legitimate.

In seeking to determine the actual weight to be assigned to the arguments in the present case, I remark, in the first place, that the method of differences is then only perfectly conclusive, when the cases compared are identical in every important respect but one. If they differ in more than one important element, the difference of result may, as far as the method of differences is concerned, be with equal justice attributed to any of these variations. So likewise, if the difference of result be not that which the presence of a new element would lead us to expect, we cannot infer that that element is inoperative, unless we are sure that its operation has not been counteracted by some of the other differences which exist between the two cases.

To show you how strongly this principle would be asserted on the other side of the question, let it be supposed that, in the case which we have been considering, the result of the statistical inquiry was different from that which it is supposed to be. Suppose it to have been proved, by an examination of the statistics of the case, that Kings do on the average live „longer than other men. Suppose now that some advocate of the doctrine of the efficacy of prayer were to adduce this fact as evidence in support of the doctrine for which he contended—what reply would be made to him? It would be said, This is not a legitimate application of the method of differences; for Kings differ from ordinary men in other respects besides the fact that more prayers are offered up for them. It may be that they are more carefully reared in their youth. It may be that they live easier lives than other men—in a word, the effect which you attribute to prayer may be due to a quite different cause. Even if no such cause can be pointed out, the phenomenon is too complex to justify you in assuming that no such cause exists. This objection seems to be reasonable.

Now the argument from the method of differences is quite as strong on the positive as on the negative side of such a question. In either case, the argument involves an assumption. Thus, on the positive side, the argument from the superior longevity of Kings (if such existed) would be—"This superior longevity is due to the prayers of their subjects, unless there be some other cause peculiar to Kings capable of producing the effect." So, if the statistics had an opposite result, the argument would be—"If prayer were really efficacious, the prayers of their subjects would give to Kings a life longer than that of ordinary men, unless there be some other cause peculiar to Kings capable of counteracting the effect." So far, the arguments are similar, and it is quite as easy to suggest, among the peculiarities of their position, causes which tend to shorten the lives of Kings as causes which tend to lengthen them.

But it is not necessary to resort to imaginary statistics to illustrate the principle of which I have spoken. Let me take a real case. There is, I suppose, no commoner subject of prayer than protection from sickness, accident, and other causes which shorten life. We may fairly assume, too, that the clergy, as a class, pray more than any other class; and yet, if any Christian controversialist were to adduce the superior longevity of the clergy as a proof of the efficacy of prayer, he would hardly be listened to. Differences favourable to longevity—as, for example, greater temperance—between the clergy and other classes would be at once pointed out. But it is quite as easy to point out class differences in the clergy unfavourable to longevity, as, for example, exposure to infectious diseases, and, despite certain threadbare sarcasms, poverty. I can see no warrant for asserting that, excluding one of the class differences, namely, prayer, the combined action of the rest would be on the whole favourable to longevity. We should be justified certainly in rejecting any supposed proof of the efficacy of prayer, derived from the greater longevity of the clergy. But we should be so justified, not because we know the other class differences to be, in their combined action, favourable to longevity—for we do not know it—but because when we know only the result of a number of causes, we cannot determine the separate action of one of them. From such knowledge we cannot prove the efficacy of the supposed cause; but I must add, neither

Argument from Statistics. 67

can we disprove it. In truth, nothing is more difficult than to find, by actual observation, two cases which satisfy the logical condition of the method of differences, by presenting a complete agreement in all important points but one. It is for this reason that we are frequently obliged, if we would apply this method with success to physical research, to have recourse to experiment, which enables us to construct artificially two cases satisfying the required condition. But in real life this condition is rarely fulfilled, on account of the complexity of the phenomena, and the number of differences which will be found to exist between almost any two cases which we can select.

The conclusion to be drawn from these observations is not, certainly, that an argument drawn from the method of differences is of no weight, unless the conditions of that method be rigorously fulfilled. Were this so, the method of differences would be of little use to us, except in the case of experiment. But it is an *argument* only; it is not a *proof;* and the weight to be assigned to it will necessarily depend upon the completeness with which these conditions are fulfilled. Every case, in which a greater supply of the blessing prayed for co-exists with a greater amount of genuine prayer, is an argument for the efficacy of prayer for that blessing, unless this greater supply can be distinctly traced to a cause independent of prayer. Every case, in which a greater amount of genuine prayer exists, without a greater supply of the blessing prayed for, is an argument against the efficacy of prayer for that blessing, unless it can be shown distinctly that a counteracting cause exists. If, in either case, the action of the other cause cannot be shown, the argument, considered as a probable argument, is valid, and its weight depends upon the improbability of the supposition that the effect is produced or counteracted by such other causes.

I could not here examine in detail the several statistical arguments which have been advanced against the efficacy of prayer. This I hope to do elsewhere;[1] for the present I would only remark that they are similar in character to the specimens which I have chosen, and that similar observations apply to them all. It is alleged, for example, as an argument against the efficacy of prayer, that the history of ships conveying missionaries, which may be supposed to command in a more than ordinary degree the prayers of the Christian Church, shows, notwithstanding, as large a percentage of wreck as that of any other ships. I do not suppose that we have any very accurate statistics on this matter: but suppose for a moment that the history of such ships *did* show a smaller percentage of wreck, and that it was proposed to found upon this fact an argument in favour of the efficacy of prayer—would it not be replied, that the induction was far too small to enable us to isolate one cause among the many which produce shipwreck. It might not be possible to deny to the argument all weight; but I am sure that the weight assigned to it would be very small. Yet it is quite as valid on the one side of the question as on the other.

We may say then of the Christian theory of prayer in its relation to Science, that it is not opposed to the general principle of Law; nor can it be refuted by experiment. The argument derived from observation is in principle

[1] Appendix, Note L.

perfectly valid, and the statistics collected by Mr. Galton and others are, on the whole, unfavourable to the theory of prayer. But the incompleteness with which the conditions of the method of differences are fulfilled obliges us to regard the argument derived from these statistics as being very far removed from proof. Let the argument be subjected to the test of which I have spoken. Imagine the statistics to be reversed. Suppose it to have been ascertained that Kings do live longer than ordinary men, and that the history of missionary ships shows a percentage of wreck less than the average. Then ask those who use the argument whether they would admit that the theory of prayer was thereby proved. I am very sure that they would refuse, and rightly, to assent to such a conclusion. They would say, It is an argument, but it is no more; and that is the truth.

I hope in my next Lecture to examine the evidence on the other side of this important question. To those, if such there be, who refuse to listen to any arguments save those drawn from observation, I can only say, Unless the argument to which you give this monopoly amount to practical demonstration, your exclusive method is not justified by reason; and you will not attain to truth if you deliberately mutilate the evidence on which it rests.

LECTURE V.

OBJECTIONS TO A THEORY OF THE WORLD WHICH EXCLUDES PRAYER.

PSALM lxv. 2.

"O Thou that hearest prayer, unto Thee shall all flesh come."

THE arguments hitherto examined have been altogether on that side of the question which is usually called the negative side. They have taken the form of objections to a system of the world which includes prayer among the causes which produce or modify phenomena. I now proceed to consider objections which may be made against a system of the world which excludes prayer from this list. I remind you that the choice must be made between these alternatives; and that scepticism, a state of mind which is admissible, and even commendable, with regard to many purely theoretic questions, is here rendered impossible, so far, at least, as our actions are concerned, by the practical character of the subject. I remind you also that, in order to conduct the inquiry without giving an undue advantage to either system, I proposed to examine, not the arguments for and against one, but either the arguments in favour of each, or the arguments against each. These methods are plainly equivalent; inasmuch as, the systems being mutually exclusive, an argument in favour of either system is an argument against the other. I have preferred the negative form for both classes of arguments, because it is in this form that arguments in favour of the system which excludes prayer have generally appeared. In other words, these arguments have usually taken the form of *objections*. It is better, therefore, that arguments in favour of the other system should be thrown into the same form; and it is in this form that I propose to consider them. These objections will have, and have had, in the estimation of men, an amount of weight varying widely with their mental constitution and beliefs. Some will appear to some minds to have no force at all. I do not speak of those who refuse to admit the existence of a God. To them, the very discussion of our present subject would be an absurdity, and I have therefore excluded Atheists from the number of those to whom these observations are addressed. But that, even among Theists, there are wide differences as to the weight to be assigned to such objections is well known, and will be apparent to you as I proceed to consider them.

The first of these objections is sufficiently obvious, whatever weight men may choose to assign to it. It seems impossible to reconcile with the teaching of Scripture a system of the world which excludes petitionary prayer. No possible system of interpretation could remove this element from the Bible. The general principle, of which prayer is one development, penetrates the entire fabric of the old dispensations. If the records of these dispensations teach anything, they teach this principle, that the actions of God towards man are, or at least were then, conditioned by the actions of man towards God. Assume the truth of a system which is the reverse of this. Assume that the actions of God are unconditioned by any actions of man which have God for their immediate object, and try to reconcile this system with the theology of the Old Testament, and you will find the task to be impossible. If it be a delusion to think that such actions of man can in anywise influence that which man receives from God, it is a delusion which is intensified by all that the Old Testament teaches of the Divine nature. That man's welfare is conditioned by some of his own actions, we all know. That man's welfare was, under the old dispensations, conditioned by actions whose immediate object was God—which had no direct tendency to procure for man the objects of his desire, and which could be supposed to affect his welfare only through the Divine will—this is the distinct teaching of the Old Testament. The Mosaic Law, for example, while it did not create the belief in the efficacy of such actions—that had existed long before—added largely to their number, and intensified the belief itself, by giving to it a formal sanction.

It is hardly necessary that I should adduce any instances in proof of this. We do not need the authority of the Epistle to the Hebrews to convince us, that sacrifice had no direct tendency to cleanse man's heart from the power of sin, or to deliver him from its consequences. Both these effects were believed to follow directly from the Divine volition, and sacrifice was but the condition which God had made essential to their production; and it is evident that sacrifice was, like prayer, an action whose immediate object was God.

If it cannot be denied that the general principle of which I have spoken finds expression in the Mosaic Law, it may, however, be contended that the particular development of this principle, with which we are at present concerned, holds a very subordinate place. Much is said of the duty of obedience; sacrifice is insisted on strongly, and in great detail; but of the duty or the efficacy of prayer we hear very little.

This is certainly true. So far as the formal exposition of the law is concerned, prayer, as we understand the word, is not strongly insisted on as a duty. But prayer as a practice, and its efficacy as a fact, find a place in the recorded lives of the best men of the Old Testament. The Jewish lawgiver himself, though he did not impress this duty very strongly upon his people, is recorded to have employed, and that successfully, on every important occasion, that kind of prayer, against which perhaps the most plausible objections may be made—I mean intercessory prayer. More than once, the intercession of Moses is recorded to have saved the Israelites from instant destruction.[1] Again and again, the calamities, which descended on their enemies in so many varied forms, are said to have been arrested by the same agency.[2] Nor is the possession of this power with God represented to be peculiar to Moses: the same is attributed to Abraham[3] and to Jacob.[4] In fact the same principle runs through the historical part

[1] Numbers, xiv. 11-20; xvi. 20-22, 44-49.   [2] Exodus, viii.-x.
[3] Genesis, xviii. 23-32.   [4] Genesis, xxxii. 28.

of the Pentateuch. Historically if not dogmatically, the doctrine of the efficacy of prayer appears in these Books with perfect distinctness. It presents itself, in fact, less as a truth to be taught and learned, than as a religious axiom which no one doubted.

The same principle finds expression in the other Books of the Old Testament. The prayers of Samuel,[1] of Elijah,[2] of Hezekiah,[3] were, if we may believe these records, not less efficacious than the prayers of Moses. The Psalms, composed at various times, are inspired by the same belief. It comforts the remorse of David.[4] It is the ray of light which penetrates the darkness of the Babylonian captivity.[5] But I do not care to dwell longer on this point, the rather because I think that it will hardly be disputed. Whether the doctrine of the efficacy of prayer be true or false, there can be, I suppose, little doubt that it is taught throughout the Old Testament. In rejecting, therefore, as false the doctrine of the efficacy of prayer, we must reject as false the teaching of the Old Testament, upon a point of the last importance.

Many would, no doubt, accept this condition without difficulty. Even among those who do not wholly deny the authority of Scripture, some might be disposed to contend that much of the teaching of the Old Testament was not intended to be permanent. That Book, or rather collection of Books, professes to record the dealing of God, not with mankind in general, but with one very peculiar nation, and under circumstances which are not likely to recur. We cannot, then, argue that, because a certain

[1] I. Samuel, xii. 18. [2] I. Kings, xvii., 21, 22; xviii. 36, 37, 38.
[3] II. Kings, xx. 2–11. [4] Psalm li. [5] Psalm cii.

Argument from Scripture—Old Testament. 75

condition was imposed upon men at that time, it is necessarily in force now. Sacrifice has passed away—why not prayer also?

This argument is to a certain extent valid. The efficacy of prayer under the Jewish dispensation would not prove its efficacy now. It would be no sufficient answer to those who simply deny the efficacy of prayer as a *fact*; although it would be quite a sufficient answer to those who deny the efficacy of prayer as being inconsistent with the Divine perfections. If we are prepared to adopt, on these grounds, a prayerless system of the world, we must be prepared also to reject the teaching of the Old Testament, as giving a false conception of the attributes of God. Many would, as I have said, accept this condition without difficulty. I only ask you to remember that it *is* the condition.

We have now to inquire—Can the credit of Scripture be saved by this hypothesis? Is the position tenable, that prayer was indeed Divinely sanctioned under the Jewish dispensation, but that, like many other things having similar authority, it passed away under the light of Christianity? Is this one of the features in the teaching of Moses, which has been effaced by the teaching of Christ?

The reply which the New Testament gives to this question is in nowise doubtful. The Founder of the Christian religion has enforced and encouraged the practice of prayer by every means which a teacher could use. In the first place, He has directly taught and enjoined it. He has done so by direct precept: "Pray that ye enter not into temptation;"[1] "Men ought always to pray and not to faint;"[2] "Pray ye that your flight be not in the winter, nor on the Sabbath-day."[3] He has done so even more forcibly when He taught His disciples *how* to pray.[4] That form of words which is the common inheritance of Christendom consists, not indeed wholly, yet so largely, of petitionary prayer, that it is impossible to avoid the conclusion, that Christ meant to teach the efficacy of such prayer.

Further, in the words which precede the institution of the Lord's Prayer, Christ enunciates, and in a certain sense adopts, one of the most favourite objections to the practice of prayer. I refer to that objection which, basing itself on the omniscience of God, regards petitionary prayer as at least superfluous—"Your Father knoweth what things ye have need of, before ye ask Him."[5] But you will remember that the use which He makes of this undoubted truth is to guide, not to abolish, the practice of petitionary prayer. "Use not vain repetitions," but "after this manner pray ye."[5] He could hardly have given His decision more plainly as to the true bearing of this objection—what it does prove, and what it does not prove. And certainly no honest teacher would set himself to improve a system which he believed to be false in its fundamental conception.

That the teaching of Christ on this subject was enforced by His own example I need hardly remind you. A single

[1] St. Matthew, xxvi. 41.
[2] St. Luke, xviii. 1.
[3] St. Matthew, xxiv. 20.
[4] St. Luke, xi. 1-4.
[5] St. Matthew, vi. 7, 8, 9.

passage such as, " He went out into a mountain to pray, and continued all night in prayer to God,"¹ is sufficient to show what value He attached to the communion of the soul with God. But here we must be careful not to draw from such a statement more than its legitimate consequence. All prayer is not petitionary prayer; and if we had not the teaching of Christ on this subject, it would not be possible to prove, from such a statement, that He had given any sanction to the use of *such* prayer. Having His teaching, however, in which the sanction is formally given, the practice of petitionary prayer being even enjoined, it would not be an unjust assumption that such prayer was included in His own communion with God, even if we had no other proof of this fact. But there *is* independent proof that this was so. Thus, for example, the recorded thanksgiving—" Father, I thank thee that thou hast heard me,"² must plainly have been elicited by the success of a previously offered petition; and the addition, "I knew that thou hearest me always," proves that the incident was not a solitary one, but that, on the contrary, petitionary prayer was with Him a usual habit.

Further, and more nearly to our present purpose, the Founder of the Christian religion not only made the duty of prayer one of its precepts, but also made the efficacy of prayer one of its doctrines. I need hardly remind you of the strong language in which it is expressed—" If ye then, being evil, know how to give good gifts unto your children, how much more shall your Father which is in Heaven give good things to them

---

¹ St. Luke, vi. 12.   ² St. John, xi. 41, 42.

that ask Him"?[1]—language indeed which, if we do not bear in mind and allow for the habitual strength of the words of Christ, might seem to express a doctrine exaggerated beyond the bounds of any possible realization; as for example, "What things soever ye desire, when ye pray, believe that ye receive them, and ye shall have them."[2]

But even more decisive than any individual text, as to the teaching of Christ upon this point, is the general tone of the language in which He speaks to His disciples of God, and of their relations to Him. The very epithet which He habitually used—"your Father"—would have been, unless He meant to teach the efficacy of prayer, necessarily misleading. If the analogy which that word expresses was not meant to be real—if Christ did not mean to teach His disciples, that in their hour of need or of sorrow they might approach God with the same feelings as those with which a child approaches an earthly parent, then the use of this epithet was in nothing short of a very cruel deceit. This alternative is, of course, not to be thought of.

On the whole, then, unless we are prepared to reject, as unauthentic, the records of Christ's teaching which remain to us, I think we are bound to accept as proved the fact, that He did teach to His disciples, and through them to the world, the doctrine of the efficacy of prayer. We cannot, then, accept a system of the world from which this element is wholly excluded, without rejecting as erroneous the teaching of Christ upon a point of the greatest impor-

---

[1] St. Matthew, vii. 11.   [2] St. Mark, xi. 24.

tance. We must believe that He gave to the community which He founded a false notion of the nature of God. Many would, as in the case of the Old Testament, accept this alternative without difficulty; but, as before, I only ask you to remember that it *is* the alternative.

The next argument, against a system of the world excluding prayer, which I proceed to consider, is that derived from the general consent of mankind.[1] To adopt a system of the world from which prayer is excluded, would be to disregard the most nearly universal of all the religious sentiments—to weed out of every system of Theism the one element in which all systems agree. What weight is to be attached to this consideration? If mankind have agreed to attribute a certain quality to the Divine Being, ought we to regard that agreement as affording a certain probability that He does really possess that quality? If, to take the present example, men have agreed to ascribe to Him a willingness to hear prayer, is this agreement to be considered evidence in favour of the reality of this attribute, or ought we to set it aside as being of little or no weight?

Before we adopt the latter alternative, which many would assent to without difficulty, let us consider what are its legitimate consequences. What is the nature of the argument derived from the general consent of mankind; and, if we should feel bound to reject it as devoid of weight, how would our beliefs generally be thereby affected? If we set aside here the general consent of mankind, not because it is overborne by other arguments, but

[1] Appendix, Note M.

because it is itself wholly unreliable, how far are we bound to extend the same scepticism to other cases?

I have already said, quoting from an eminent modern writer, that with us the criterion of ultimate truth is simply the impossibility of disbelieving it. We believe, because we cannot help it. We adopt a certain conclusion, because our minds are, by their own constitution, irresistibly urged to this conclusion. If the force which thus urges us be irresistible, we regard the conclusion as certain. If the force be not absolutely irresistible, but only very great— if disbelief be not impossible, but only very difficult—we regard the conclusion as probable only. Sometimes this impossibility, or difficulty, of refusing assent is felt immediately; sometimes it is not felt until the mind has passed through the preliminary stage of apprehending and examining the proofs or arguments which are advanced in support of the conclusion. But in either case, the ultimate test of truth, certain or probable, is, for us, the impossibility or difficulty of believing the reverse.

In the second case, where belief in the reverse of the conclusion is not impossible, but only difficult, this difficulty, and therefore our assurance of the truth of the conclusion itself, is enhanced, necessarily and rightly, by the fact that the same difficulty has presented itself to a large number of other minds. For the question must force itself on our consideration, How is this agreement to be accounted for? Why have so many minds found a difficulty in believing the opposite to this conclusion? If the difficulty were present to a few minds only, we might suppose the existence of something exceptional in their constitutions; but if the agreement be general, if in the great majority of minds, and in minds of every variety, the conclusion satisfies the condition which is to us the ultimate criterion of probable truth, I do not see how, on any principle short of universal scepticism, we can deny to such a conclusion the title of probable; unless there be within our knowledge some cause (a moral prejudice, for example) wholly unconnected with the *truth* of the conclusion, which may account for the general agreement which has been observed. If there be such a cause, the proof of its existence in the minds of any number of men ought to diminish the weight to be assigned to their agreement. If the cause be universally present, its existence ought to diminish the confidence which we place either in our own judgment, or in that of other men; and might even suggest scepticism as the appropriate attitude for a philosophic mind. But if this attitude be impossible, as in practical questions it must be, we must then decide by the only ultimate test—difficulty of disbelief.

You will observe that I have taken as the criterion of probable truth, not the facility with which the mind believes the conclusion itself, but the difficulty which it finds in believing the opposite. I have done so, because this difficulty of disbelief appears to me to express clearly the attitude which the mind assumes towards a conclusion which we call probable. But perhaps I ought to add a few words for the purpose of explaining to you the sense in which I use the phrase "difficulty of disbelief." When we speak of a proposition as certain, we mean, I suppose, that no force of reasoning or evidence which we can conceive it possible to adduce would change the attitude of our minds from belief into disbelief. We think the proposition to be true, and we cannot conceive a mental condition in which we should think otherwise. When we speak of a proposition as highly probable only, we mean that it would require a large force of evidence to change the attitude of our minds, but that such a change is not inconceivable. In the first case, disbelief is impossible; in the second case it is only difficult, in a degree varying with the probability of the proposition itself. I do not here speak of the *grounds* of probability, but of the state of the mind itself, considered in relation to the proposition which it regards as probable.

I have now to inquire how far we are justified in inferring difficulty of disbelief from the mere fact of belief. If we know, as a matter of fact, that men believe a proposition, have we a right to assume that they would find it difficult to disbelieve it? Not in all cases, certainly. Men give, not unfrequently, an indolent assent to an assertion which may happen to come under their notice, and yet it is impossible not to see, that they would have assented quite as readily to an opposite statement if it had been presented to them. From such a belief you cannot infer difficulty of disbelief; nor therefore can you found upon it any argument in support of the probability of the conclusion. Generally speaking, however, we *may* presume difficulty of disbelief from the fact of belief; and we may always do so, when the question is such that a right decision is a matter of practical importance. Here, it is highly improbable that the assent is careless, and therefore also improbable—almost impossible—that the mind would with equal facility have assented to an opposite statement if presented to it. And if it should appear that the mind, in arriving at the belief in question, had distinctly before it the possibility that the opposite conclusion might be the true one, this latter supposition is plainly inadmissible. If, then, we find a general agreement among men upon a question in the right decision of which they are deeply interested, and in which both sides have been, most probably, under their consideration, we may fairly assume that they would have found a difficulty in coming to an opposite conclusion. I do not think, therefore, that we can reject the argument in favour of the truth of the conclusion which may be derived from such an agreement, without general scepticism as to man's power of arriving at probable truth. What amount of actual weight ought to be assigned to such an argument is another and a very difficult question. I can only suggest some considerations tending to the solution.

But in the first place, let me endeavour to justify the assertion that we cannot wholly reject, on any principles short of universal scepticism, the argument drawn from the general agreement of mankind. We find that men generally agree in a certain conclusion. That is the phenomenon to be accounted for. Is the truth of the conclusion a mode of accounting for this agreement? If it be not, we must suppose the human mind to be indifferent as between truth and falsehood, and this supposition is equivalent to general scepticism. If there be in the human mind a tendency to prefer truth to falsehood, the agreement of mankind *does* raise a presumption in favour of the truth of the conclusion in which they agree; and the evidential value of this agreement is much enhanced, if the question be of such a kind that we are warranted in assuming that all or most of those who believe the conclusion would have found it difficult to believe the contrary.

How shall we know that we *may* assume this? How shall we distinguish between that indolent, careless assent which, but for some accident, might as well have been dissent—which some cause as slight might change into dissent; or, it may be, born of ignorance, to vanish like other spectres of the darkness before the growing light of knowledge—and that far other assent, the expression of a deeply-seated belief, not perhaps unchangeable, yet hard to change—an assent which we *may* find to be erroneous, which is certainly not infallible; but to which, I repeat, we can deny all weight only by that complete distrust in the human faculties which has no consistent result but universal scepticism?

One kind of valueless assent, that, namely, which springs from indolence, we have seen already how to exclude. How to exclude the valueless assent which has its root in ignorance or prejudice—for that problem, alas, there is no complete solution. We can detect the ignorance or the prejudice of other times, but who shall teach us to unmask the ignorance or the prejudice of our own time?

Yet even if we cannot find a complete solution of the problem, we must try to solve it, at least partially, if we would not abandon the pursuit of truth as hopeless. And in this very phenomenon of general agreement we shall find, I think, a partial solution.

The general agreement of mankind to accept a conclusion as true is a phenomenon which we must try to account for. Now to account for a general phenome-

Argument from General Assent.

non we must look for a general cause—something which not only acts generally, but acts always or generally in the same direction. The truth of the conclusion is such a cause. We cannot, as I have said, deny, on any principle short of universal scepticism, that men are more disposed to believe a true conclusion than a false one. The truth of the conclusion is therefore *a* method of accounting for the agreement of mankind to accept it. If we propose to account for the agreement in any other way, as by ignorance or prejudice, we are bound to show not only that the cause which we select operates generally, but that it would influence men generally in the same direction. If this cannot be shown, there is a presumption in favour of the cause which *is* general in its operation, namely, the truth of the conclusion.

This presumption is greatly strengthened, when we can actually trace the general agreement to one of those common principles of human nature, whose authority we always recognise in our search after truth. If the general belief of which we speak be founded on such a principle, it is plain that disbelief, which requires us to reject its authority, could not be otherwise than difficult. In such a case, then, the criterion of probability already spoken of would be satisfied. In a word, the generality of the agreement excludes an *accidental* cause. We must seek its origin in some general principle of human nature. Such an origin already establishes a presumption in favour of the truth of that which men have agreed to believe; and if, further, we can show that the principle to which this agreement owes its origin is one of those to which we usually accord authority, the presumption is very greatly strengthened. For we may fairly assume, that men who believe on such grounds would find it very difficult to disbelieve.

I should now proceed to inquire whether, and how far, these principles are applicable to our present subject—the general agreement among men on the practice, and therefore the efficacy, of prayer. I hope in my next Lecture to consider this question, the examination of which will nearly bring the present inquiry to a close.

LECTURE VI.

ARGUMENT AGAINST A SYSTEM OF THE WORLD WHICH EXCLUDES PRAYER, DERIVED FROM THE GENERAL ASSENT OF MANKIND—RECAPITULATION.

St. Matthew, vi. 9.

"Our Father, which art in Heaven."

IN my last Lecture I endeavoured, as you may remember, to make some advance towards a solution of the question, What evidential weight ought we to assign to the agreement of mankind? We saw that the agreement ought to be general, so as to exclude the supposition that it is induced by any peculiarity, either of time or place; and that it ought to be capable of being traced, at least with probability, to some of those principles which we recognise as authoritative; so as to exclude, as far as we can exclude, an agreement which is the result of prejudice.

I now proceed to inquire whether, and how far, these conditions are fulfilled by the agreement which exists among men on the subject of prayer. And, in the first place, Is the agreement general? To this question there can be but one answer. Prayer is, and has ever been, an element of every system of Theism—of the polytheism of the Greeks and Romans, no less than of the monotheism of the Jews—of the religious systems of Zoroaster and of Mahomet, no less than of the religion of Christ. The spirit of prayer breathes through the hymns to Indra and Varuna no less really than through the Psalms of David. The phenomenon is quite general; and the cause must be sought, not in any accidental peculiarity, but in some principle spreading as widely as human nature itself. So far the condition is fulfilled.

In truth, the cause of the general agreement among all systems of Theism on the subject of prayer is to be found in the agreement on this point of all these systems in their conceptions of the nature of the Divine Being. These conceptions are indeed, in many respects, widely different. It would seem almost profane to institute a comparison between the portrait drawn by Christianity, and the portrait drawn by Paganism. But they have this element in common—All these systems, how widely soever they differ in other respects, agree in depicting the Divine Being as one who is willing to listen to the prayers of His creatures. If, as in the Polytheistic systems, there be more than one Divine Being, this characteristic is shared by them all.

But our question is not yet answered. For we have still to inquire, Whence comes *this* agreement? Why do portraits of the Divine Nature, drawn by religious systems so many and so various, agree in presenting the same feature? Only two causes, I think, can be assigned, sufficiently general to account for the phenomenon— general experience, and a moral intuition. As it is cer-

Argument from the Moral Sense. 89

tainly not the first, we must seek the origin of this feature, common to all portraitures of the Divine Nature, in a general moral intuition. It is man's moral sense which has drawn the picture. It is man's moral sense which tells him, that, among the qualities which in their aggregate make up such a character as man can venerate, readiness to comply, if possible, with the desire of a suppliant, is one. An inexorable being is not man's ideal of moral perfection; and accordingly the history of the world tells us that such a character has never been his ideal of God.

If you refuse to attribute this historical phenomenon to a moral instinct, how do you propose to account for it? What cause can be assigned sufficiently powerful and sufficiently general to account for the phenomenon?

This conception of the Divine Nature, it will be answered by many, is unreliable, because it is anthropomorphic. Your God is only an exaggerated man. You have transferred, without authority, to your conception of the Divine Nature elements which properly belong only to the nature of man. It is in nowise surprising that there should be agreement among portraits drawn from the same original. But what inference can be deduced from such agreement?

If, by the assertion that our conception of God is anthropomorphic, it be meant that our portrait is a mere copy —that we have transferred the elements of a human character in the aggregate, and without selection, to our conception of God—the assertion is not true. If it be meant that we have formed our ideal of the Divine Nature by a selection of human qualities, including some and omitting others, I am not concerned to dispute the truth of this theory; on the contrary, I believe it to be correct. But the question at once presents itself, On what principle has the selection been made? Why have we included some human qualities in our conception of the Divine Nature, and excluded others? There seems to be but one answer to this question. We have included good qualities, and excluded bad ones; in other words, we have been guided in the selection by a moral instinct. This is in effect the same account of the matter with that already given. The moral instinct of man is not indeed infallible; and there will be found in some of the conceptions which men have formed of the Divine Nature elements which are not good. It must be remembered, however, that we are not now concerned with exceptional cases, but with an element which is common to all, or nearly all, the conceptions which man has formed of God.

If, therefore, we resolve to adopt, as true, a system of the world from which prayer is excluded, we must either admit that the world is governed by a Being who is not good; or we must reject the all but universal verdict of man's moral sense, that desire to comply with the prayer of a suppliant is a necessary element of a benevolent nature.

In the earlier part of the present discussion, I alluded to an argument sometimes advanced on the other side of the question, professedly derived from the same source with the present argument, namely, the conception which we ought to form of the Divine Nature. I endeavoured to examine this argument on its own merits, without inquiring into the prevalence of the conception of moral excellence on which it is founded. I may now add, appropriately to the present stage of the discussion, that this

Stoic ideal never has been generally accepted. It has been a paradox, professed by very few, and which the moral sense of mankind in general has refused to accept as a picture of excellence either in God or man.

Hitherto I have considered the argument drawn from the general agreement of mankind purely in its metaphysical aspect, without the intermixture of any Theistic element. Returning now into the region of Theism, I proceed to inquire how this argument is affected by the belief that man's moral nature, like the rest of the universe, is the work of a Divine Creator.

Reliance on the efficacy of prayer, considered as a general phenomenon of human nature, is founded, as we have seen, in a common element pervading all the conceptions which man has formed of the Supreme Being. Particular classes of men—Christians, for example—have other and special reasons for this belief; but the general reason, which we are bound to seek for a general phenomenon, is, that absolute indifference to prayer is not reconcileable with the conceptions which men in general have formed of God. Man's moral nature appears to be such, that whenever it would draw a picture of ideal perfection—or in other words, a picture of God—it has made compassion, evoked by prayer, one of the features of its portrait. If this portrait be untrue, we must suppose that God has given to man a moral nature which is all but universally unreliable in a matter so deeply important as the character of God Himself, and the attitude which man ought to assume towards Him.

The moral judgment of man is not indeed infallible; but if it can err, all but universally, in such a matter as this—if men can agree to call that a moral excellence which is a moral fault, where can their moral sense be trusted? Is not the legitimate result of such a supposition the worst of all scepticisms—moral scepticism? And if man's moral judgment be right—if desire to comply with the wish of a suppliant *be* a moral excellence, what system of Theism can exclude it from the ideal of God?

Before concluding the examination of the arguments on this side of the question, there is yet one upon which I wish to say a few words; although its scope is limited, and many would, I suppose, dispute its reality. It is the argument from what is commonly called "Christian experience." The fact upon which this argument is based is this:—There are few practical Christians who will not tell you that it has occurred to them at times to feel that their prayers *have been* answered. Perhaps they have faltered in the hour of danger; temptation has assailed them, and they have felt themselves to be weak. They have sought the aid of their Father who is in Heaven, and their courage has sprung up anew. The temptation but now so formidable has passed by harmless; and they will tell you that the effect has been produced, not by anything in themselves, but by an external power, and in immediate answer to their prayer.

The scope of this argument is, as I have said, limited. It does not extend beyond the efficacy of prayer for spiritual blessings. But as we have already seen that the *à priori* objections to prayer for temporal blessings lie equally against prayer for spiritual blessings, it is plain that the argument, considered in its bearing upon objections of this class, is quite general, if it be real. But many will dispute the reality, not indeed of the facts, but of the inference which is drawn from them. They will say that these facts are a proof of the power of prayer, not over the mind of God, but over the mind of the individual who prays. They will say that these facts indicate no more than the natural efficacy of a strong desire to produce the desired result, if that result be mental. You believe, they will say, that your heart has been purified, or your power of resisting temptation strengthened, by prayer; and so, indeed, it has been—not because prayer has procured for you the aid of the Divine grace, but because the earnest desire which has found expression in prayer has, by its own natural power, purified or strengthened your heart. That this is a *possible* explanation of the phenomenon, there can be, I think, no doubt. It is not impossible that the effect may be produced by the reflex action of prayer on the mind; if it were, we should be absolutely compelled to adopt the other explanation, and these facts would be decisive in favour of the efficacy of prayer for spiritual blessings. But while we cannot call this interpretation impossible, nor even, considered in its own nature, improbable, we must remember that it would not be accepted by those who have the best means of judging—those, namely, in whose minds the effect is produced. They would tell you that they can distinguish perfectly between the effect of an unexpressed desire, however earnest, and the effect of the same desire poured out to God. If you say that the whole phenomenon is due to the firm belief, admittedly present to their minds, that their prayers will be answered, and that from this to the further belief that their prayers *have* been answered, the transition is easy; they will refuse to accept a theory of the phenomenon which implies that this latter belief is a delusion of their own minds. They will say that, like many other metaphysical theories, capable of plausible statement, it is opposed to their inner consciousness, and that therefore they must reject it as untrue.

Now, it is quite true that they may be deceived. Their consciousness may have reported untruly; or they may have mistaken for the testimony of consciousness something which was an inference, and an erroneous inference, of their reason. But unless we are prepared to reject altogether the evidence of man with regard to that which passes within him, and with it the foundation of all mental science, we cannot refuse to such an argument as this a certain amount of weight.

I have thus endeavoured to lay before you, as fully as the space allotted to me would permit, the arguments on both sides of this great question. I have not knowingly omitted any, although, no doubt, many considerations have suggested themselves to you which I have failed to notice. But before I try to bring together in one picture the opposing probabilities which we have severally examined, I must supply one omission which the course of the argument compelled me to make, and which leaves the discussion still somewhat incomplete.

You may remember that, in commenting upon a certain experiment which has been proposed for the purpose of testing the efficacy of prayer, I pointed out to you that, assuming the result of the experiment to be as anticipated, we could not argue from that result against the efficacy of prayer in general, but only against the efficacy of prayer tried as an experiment. And I said that any person holding the Christian theory of prayer would predict the result of such an experiment. It is objected to this answer—You do but degrade your conception of God, if you suppose that He would frustrate an experiment made with the honest purpose of eliciting the truth; and if this be the Christian theory, so much the worse for Christianity. The objection is both obvious and plausible. I proceed to consider it.

It is true that the Christian theory of prayer would predict the failure of such an experiment. It is true that the Christian religion teaches us that trust in God is the condition, not the result, of successful prayer. It *is* the teaching of Christianity that he who comes to God in prayer must believe that "He is a rewarder of them that diligently seek Him." Is such a condition unworthy of the character of God?

I remind you here of an observation before made in discussing the question, What is the peculiar claim of a suppliant? Why do we prefer one who asks for our assistance to another, equally deserving in other respects, who does not ask for it? We saw then that the element which justifies this preference is trust. We prefer one who asks, because the request itself implies trust. But if we knew that this element was not present, and that the request was only an experiment, I do not think that we should be at all inclined to give a preference to such a suppliant. In fact, there would be no reason for such a preference. So, too, prayer to God offered without trust has no special claim on His mercy. He who prays thus has no right to expect that he will be preferred to one who does not pray at all.

But it may still be urged, Is not the purpose of prayer in the supposed experiment a good purpose? Is not he who offers the prayer actuated by a sincere desire to elicit the truth? And why should God baffle the purpose of an honest inquirer, even if he be not possessed of the Christian grace of faith?

But the answer is obvious. Because, if God did comply with such a prayer, he would simply lead the honest inquirer astray. The success of the supposed experiment would prove, not simply the efficacy of prayer, but the efficacy of prayer *without faith*. If the Christian theory of prayer be true, this conclusion is untrue; and if God were to grant success to such a prayer, He would lead men to expect that which He did not mean to give them.

But it is time that this discussion should approach to a close. Little indeed remains, but that I should take a brief retrospect of the question as I have endeavoured to present it to you, before I leave the decision to the judgment of your own minds.

Two principles—neither, I think, doubtful—were originally adopted to govern the investigation; one, that the question belongs to that practical class, where scepticism is impossible, and the mind is compelled to come to a decision; the other, that any attempt to decide the question upon one kind of evidence ought to be rejected as illogical, unless the evidence to which it is proposed to accord this monopoly have the force of demonstration.

The task which is here set before us—the task which every man must perform, by his life, if not by his words—

Recapitulation.

is to decide between a system of the world which includes prayer, and a system of the world which excludes it. To assist you in making this decision, without giving, in form, any advantage to either side, I have presented to you the arguments for and against the efficacy of prayer as *objections* against these systems respectively.

Objections against a system of the world including prayer among its efficient causes are derived, as we have seen, principally from three sources: from a certain conception of the Divine Nature; from the principle of Law; and from experience.

Examining these objections successively, I endeavoured to show you that the Stoic ideal, on which the first objection is founded, ought to be rejected as being inconsistent with the moral sense; and that, as a matter of fact, the vast majority of mankind have refused to accept it as a portrait of moral excellence, either in God or man.

I endeavoured to show you, further, that although it is true that, in asking God to interfere, either in the world of spirit or in the world of matter, we ask Him to perform a miracle, it is not true that we ask for a violation of the principle of Law; and that the "dogma of interference," when rightly understood, is in nowise derogatory to the character of God, regarded as the Creator and Ruler of the world.

Passing from the *a priori* arguments against the efficacy of prayer to those which are based upon experience, we found that these are of two kinds, namely, arguments drawn from experiment, and arguments drawn from observation; the scope of both being limited to the efficacy of prayer in the physical world. I endeavoured to show

H

you that the first class ought to be set aside, as being made under conditions inconsistent with the requirements of the theory which it is meant to test.

But with regard to the argument from observation, it is impossible to deny either its soundness or its applicability to a question like the present. I have not attempted to dispute either. But I have pointed out to you the difficulty and uncertainty (an uncertainty which has, indeed, become proverbial) introduced into the application of this argument, by the complexity of the facts with which it has to deal, and by the very imperfect manner in which the conditions of the method of differences, on which this argument is based, are fulfilled. These observations were meant to show, not that the argument is without weight, but that it is very far from being decisive. And I asked you, before fixing the amount of weight which you would allow to any such argument on the negative side, to imagine the statistics to be reversed, and then to consider what weight you would assign to the argument thus transferred to the positive side.

Passing now from objections against a system of the world which includes prayer, to objections against a system of the world which excludes it, I pointed out to you that the adoption of this latter system would compel us to reject wholly the teaching of Scripture. If prayer forms no part of the conditions by which the action of the Supreme Being is determined, then it must be confessed that "Moses and the prophets" give us a very false idea of the Divine nature. If the Divine volition cannot be influenced, or at least conditioned, by human actions having God for their object, the Theistic teaching of the patriarchal and Mosaic systems must be regarded as radically false.

I reminded you also that that which is true of the teaching of Moses is no less true of the teaching of Christ. If we *are* constrained to reject the theory which includes prayer among the causes which produce or modify phenomena, we must also reject the teaching of Christ as, on this point, wholly erroneous; we must admit that the Founder of the Christian religion gave to His disciples, and through them to the Christian Church, the same false notion of the nature of God which Moses and the prophets had given before Him. And as we must suppose Him to have been wrong in His teaching, so must we suppose Him to have been wrong also in His life. For, if there be truth in the history which remains to us, it is plain that, as He taught, so He lived, and so He died.

We saw, further, that a system of the world which excludes prayer is opposed to the universal religious sentiment of mankind. A prayerless Theism has found favour with so few, that it may almost be said that it has never existed. If, therefore, we accept a theory of the world which excludes prayer, we must reject an intuition of man's moral nature which is all but universal. We must suppose those portraits of Divine perfection, which man's moral nature has drawn, to be erroneous in that feature in which they all agree. I showed you, by an examination of our ultimate test of truth, that although other evidence may compel us to decide against this general agreement of mankind, we cannot refuse to allow it weight —even very considerable weight—on any principle short of universal scepticism.

The comparison of the two systems of the world which we have been considering is not complete without an examination of the moral effects of each. If it can be said of two rival systems that the one can satisfy certain moral wants of man's nature which the other leaves unsatisfied, or that the one would foster the growth of moral virtues which would be blighted by the other, I do not see how any Theist can deny that such a difference would raise a strong presumption in favour of the first. If the system of the world and man's moral nature have come from the same Author, it is not unreasonable to expect a harmony between them. It is not probable, surely, that a benevolent Being would implant in His creature moral desires absolutely inconsistent with the system of the world in which he lives.

You will understand that, retaining the limitation with which I commenced, I speak but of the moral wants of the Theist. What are they? What moral wants are awakened in the nature of man, when his reason has told him of the existence of God? Hear its expression in the two words which I have prefixed to this Lecture—the first words of that wondrous prayer which seems so truly to reflect the nature of its Author—so Divine and yet so human—those words which breathe to God the first moral want of the Theist's nature—" Our Father." Words the most familiar to every one among us—so familiar, indeed, that we often forget the weighty truth which they suggest, if they cannot be said to contain it—that the first want awakened in man's moral nature by belief in the existence of God is, that these words should embody a real feeling. And no system of the world will satisfy the wants of man's moral nature, which does not permit man to approach God with feelings of which these words are the truthful exponent.

Would such feelings be possible under a system from which prayer was banished? Would such feelings be evoked by a Being, whose individual will, if such a thing ever existed, has long since ceased to act—abandoning the universe, of which He might continue in name the Governor, to a series of unintelligent causes, established indeed by Him once for all, but thenceforward acting as independently of Him as if He had ceased to exist?

Take the analogous case. What would be the moral effect of a like system introduced into the things of this earth, and the part which the will of man enacts there? What if all acts of individual kindness—all promptings of individual mercy—those bright spots in our existence upon which giver and receiver alike look back so fondly—were replaced by one uniform and gigantic system—doing as much, perhaps more, good, but doing it quite irrespectively of any individual feeling—established once and for ever, and thenceforward pursuing its appointed course, changeless and inexorable as a physical law? What if it were our duty, giving our labour or our money to the support of this great system, to pass through life heedless of individual suffering, deaf to the cry of individual sorrow? What if such a system were to take possession of our homes? What if it were the duty of the parent, having made the wisest arrangements for the welfare of his children, to say to them, "All this has been done for you; and now remember that, whatever be your need, whatever trouble may assail you, you must not look to me for help"? And what if the parent's heart were so changed, that this duty should be possible to him? Ask yourselves, Are the moral wants of the child's nature to be satisfied thus. Ask yourselves, how long love could survive under such a system. What provisions, be they never so wise—what advantages, be they never so great, could efface from the child's heart the one withering thought, that in his hour of sorrow he had sought his father, and that he would not hear? There is no difference in kind between the love of man and the love of God; and that which would blight in our hearts the love of an earthly parent would be no less fatal to the love of "Our Father who is in Heaven."

If, therefore, a system of the world from which prayer is excluded be the true one, it must be admitted that we live under a system which leaves important moral wants of our nature unsatisfied, and which would render the love of God nearly impossible. And without the love of God religion is an unreal mockery.

Is the world indeed a vast machine, and no more? If it had an intelligent Author, has His work long since ceased? Is the difference between Theism and Atheism only a matter of speculative curiosity? Is the action of the human spirit the sole exception (if it *be* an exception) to the otherwise uncontrolled power of purely physical causes? Is God the Governor of the world in this sense only, that at an epoch immeasurably remote He established these causes, intended thenceforward to act by themselves? Is He now, for all practical purposes, as completely non-existent as the Buddhist deity who has attained Nirvana?

Conclusion. 103

Or, if we do not deny Him all action—if the "dogma of interference" be not wholly untrue—is that interference determined by reasons of which the desire of His creatures is not one? Are the words "Our Father which art in Heaven" but an unmeaning sound?

This is the question which you *must* decide. Between a system of the world which includes prayer, and a system which excludes it, neutrality is impossible. If you would perform rightly that inevitable task, you must decide, not by a partial examination of the evidence, but by a review of the whole. If you decide by any other rule, if you give a monopoly to that kind of evidence—science, moral sentiment, the Bible—which your habit of thought may lead you to prefer, your method is wholly indefensible. You may attain truth, but you will attain it only by accident.

I said at the commencement of these Lectures, that I wished our consideration of this subject to take the form of an inquiry. As such I have endeavoured to conduct it, and as such I would leave it; reminding you that the question which your hearts and lives must answer is, not whether a belief in the efficacy of prayer is unattended by difficulties; not whether the opposing argument (I think we have seen that there is but one) can be completely answered; but whether that argument, to which it is impossible to deny weight, is sufficient to outweigh the teaching of the Bible, the teaching of Christ, and the moral sentiment of mankind.

APPENDIX.

Note A, Page 1.

IMPOSSIBILITY OF MAINTAINING A SCEPTICAL ATTITUDE WITH REGARD TO RELIGION.

"In questions of difficulty, or such as are thought so, where more satisfactory evidence cannot be had, or is not seen; if the result of the examination be, that there appears, upon the whole, any the lowest presumption on one side, and none on the other, or a greater presumption on one side, though in the lowest degree greater; this determines the question, even in matters of speculation; and in matters of practice will lay us under an absolute and formal obligation, in point of prudence and of interest, to act upon that presumption or low probability, though it be so low as to leave the mind in very great doubt which is the truth."—*Analogy of Religion*, pp. 5, 6 (Fitzgerald's edition).

The obligation of which Butler here speaks, attaching to matters of practice as distinguished from matters of speculation, appears to be founded on the principle stated in the text, namely, the impossibility of maintaining, in practice, a sceptical attitude. If such an attitude were possible—if in such a case we *could* act, neither as if we believed a certain statement to be true, nor as if we believed it to be false, but as if we did not know whether it were true or false, I think that such a course of action might, under certain circumstances, be the right one. In matters of speculation, where suspense of judgment *is* possible, we often—and quite reasonably—refuse to decide the question, if the preponderance of evidence be very small.

When, therefore, Butler says that such a preponderance "determines the question in matters of speculation," I think that we must understand his statement with the reservation—unless the mind may reasonably refuse to decide the question at all. But in matters of practice, where the suspense of judgment is usually impossible, and men are reduced to the alternative of acting, either in accordance with or against a small preponderance of evidence, the "formal obligation" of which Butler speaks is an undoubted reality. It must be remembered, however, in the application of this principle, that there are religious questions which are not, in this sense, practical questions, and that in dealing with such, the mind may, when the evidence is slight, reasonably suspend its decision. Of such questions I have given an example in the text (pp. 5, 6).

Note B, Page 8.

OBJECTION TO A STATEMENT OF THE QUESTION AS LYING SIMPLY BETWEEN OPPOSING PROBABILITIES.

The statement in the text, that the duty of an inquirer into the truth of the Christian doctrine of prayer is to determine between two opposing probabilities, may be thought to be unduly favourable to those who hold the negative side of the question. It may be contended that the present is one of those cases alluded to by Butler, in which it is the duty of a prudent man to act as if a certain proposition were true, even though the probability be that it is untrue. When the injury which would result from a mistake on one side is much greater than that which would result from a mistake on the other, it may be the duty of a prudent man to decide by the magnitude rather than by the probability of the result, and to accept the greater probability of the lesser evil, rather than the lesser probability of the greater evil. This principle is indisputable. In the case of an apparently hopeless illness, no father will hesitate to call in a physician, although the probabilities may be as a hundred to one that the physician can do no good. He will do so because he prefers the almost certain loss of money to the bare possibility that he may be leaving his child to die. Now it may be contended that the present is such a case. For, it will be said, if prayer be not efficacious, the man who prays is, at worst, only losing his time : whereas, if prayer be efficacious, the man who does not pray is neglecting an ordinance of God, and, it may be, forfeiting a blessing which he might otherwise have secured. It may be contended, therefore, that although as a matter of speculation the question must be decided simply between opposing probabilities, yet that, as a matter of practice, arguments on the positive side ought to have a preference over arguments of equal strength on the negative side.

This reasoning would be conclusive, if it were certainly true that loss of time is the only evil which could attend the practice of prayer, if prayer were without efficacy. But this is not certain. In the first place, there is always danger in an unreal hope. Reliance upon external assistance is generally attended by some danger that our own exertions may be relaxed; and if the reliance be groundless, this danger is not compensated by any corresponding advantage. It may, no doubt, be replied, that the exertions of the Christian are not relaxed by his reliance on Divine aid, because he knows that without such exertions he will not be granted the aid which he seeks. This is certainly true of those who have a full and practical belief in the Christian doctrine of prayer, but it is not true of all those who simply accept the efficacy of prayer as a fact; and it would be, I think, difficult to deny, that the effect of a delusive belief in this tenet would be, on the whole, like the effect of most delusive beliefs, injurious. It is, however, probable that the injury, thus caused to the energy of human exertion, would be less than that which would result from the neglect of a powerful aid, which is within man's reach, if the doctrine be true. This probability, if conceded, would tend to justify a preference, in practice, of arguments on the positive side of the question.

But there are arguments against prayer, which would refuse to admit that loss of time or relaxation of energy are the only evils which could result from this practice. In all that class of objections which I have called theological, being founded on the supposed inconsistency of a belief in the efficacy of prayer with a just conception of the Divine attributes, even the *innocence* of the practice of prayer would be denied. If these arguments be well founded, we cannot pray without forming an unworthy conception of God, and thus dishonouring Him, as far as our thoughts can dishonour Him. I have endeavoured to show that the theological arguments have little weight, but this could not be assumed at the outset. I have, therefore, in conformity with the usual custom, stated the question as one between opposing probabilities, without making any difference between the theoretical and the practical solutions. But the objection to this mode of dealing with the question is so far valid, that if the theological arguments against prayer were set aside, the philosophic arguments on the same side ought greatly to outweigh all that can be offered on the other side of the question, before they can be permitted to determine the actions of a prudent man.

NOTE C, PAGE 12.

ATTRIBUTES OF THE DEITY.

Mr. Herbert Spencer has given a negative answer to the question, whether man can form any conception of the Divine attributes, and therefore, by necessary consequence, to the further question, whether he ought to make the attempt. Such attempts are, he thinks, a barrier to the complete reconciliation between Religion and Science, which he anticipates, but which cannot be reached, until Religion admits that the mystery which she contemplates is absolutely inscrutable. And this abandonment of the effort to *know* need not, he thinks, be accompanied by any decay in the religious sentiment. Nay rather, the sentiment will take a wider and nobler form when set free from the trammels which these false conceptions have thrown around it.[1]

Are these propositions true? Is it true that the Divine Nature is absolutely inscrutable by man? Are man's conceptions of the Divine Nature at best so imperfect, that he ought to give up all attempts to form them? And would the religious sentiment gain in breadth and nobleness by this surrender?

Is the Divine Being absolutely unknowable by man? This question is ambiguous. It may mean either—Can we know God as He is in Himself? or—Can we know Him in His relation to us?

Now, there can be no doubt as to the answer which we must make to the question, if understood in the first sense. In the

[1] *First Principles*, Part I.

ordinary sense of the word "know," we can *not* know God—whatever meaning we may attach to that Name—as He is in Himself. But the same may be said of every object of our knowledge. We know nothing of things as they are in themselves, as distinguished from the effects which they produce on our minds. All our knowledge is relative—relative to our own powers of reasoning or perception. "The conviction," says Mr. Spencer, "that human intelligence is incapable of absolute knowledge is one that has been slowly gaining ground as civilization has advanced. Each new ontological theory, from time to time propounded in lieu of previous ones shown to be untenable, has been followed by a new criticism leading to a new scepticism. All possible combinations have been one by one tried and found wanting; and so the entire field of speculation has been gradually exhausted without positive result: the only result arrived at being the negative one above stated—that the reality existing beyond all appearances is, and must ever be, unknown."[1] Objects external to ourselves are known to us only as *causes* which act upon our senses and, through them, upon our intelligence, either directly or through the intervention of other objects. An object which is incapable of such causality is unknowable by us. The Uncausing, if we may use the word, must be to us for ever unknown.

But surely this cannot be said of the Divine Being. He cannot be described as The Uncausing, Who is the Ultimate Cause of all things.[2] When, therefore, we speak of Him as The Absolute, we must understand by that epithet The Uncaused, not The Uncausing. Whatever relativity attaches to the word "cause," the same relativity attaches to the Ultimate Cause; and it is precisely this relativity which brings the Divine

[1] *First Principles*, pp. 68, 69.
[2] This latter epithet is adopted by Mr. Spencer himself: *First Principles*, pp. 108–9.

Attributes of the Deity.

Being in some degree within the sphere of human knowledge. The relativity of all our knowledge excludes us from all knowledge of the Uncausing; but no similar impossibility opposes itself to our knowledge of the Uncaused. Mr. Spencer uses the word "absolute" as synonymous with "non-relative."[1] If this latter term, in its proper sense, were applicable to the Divine Being, the relativity of all our knowledge would render that Being absolutely unknowable by us. But I do not see how the term "non-relative" can properly be applied to a *cause*. The very name denotes a relation. But if a cause *may* be described as non-relative, the non-relative is not unknowable. For it is evident that no cause is absolutely unknown to us of which we know *any* of the effects. If we know these effects imperfectly, or if the effects which we know be small in number, compared with those of which we are ignorant, our knowledge of the cause is imperfect—in the latter case very imperfect—but, as far as it goes, real. In truth it is the only *kind* of knowledge which we can possess. We know an external cause only by the effects which it produces, either directly on ourselves, or indirectly by the production of external phenomena, which in their turn affect us. The most perfect knowledge of a cause which we can possess is no more than knowledge of all the effects which it is capable of producing. If it be capable of producing a thousand effects, and if we know them all, our knowledge is perfect; or, to speak more accurately, it is as nearly perfect as our present faculties appear to permit. If we know but one, our knowledge is very imperfect. Still it is real as far as it goes, and must not be confounded with absolute ignorance.

It must be remembered that the word "cause" is here used rather in a popular than in a strictly scientific sense. Strictly speaking, the word "cause" is applied to the whole combination

[1] *First Principles*, p. 91.

necessary to produce a given effect; and in this sense a cause can have but one effect. But in a popular sense we use the word "cause" to denote some important element entering into many different combinations, and profoundly modifying the effect which the other elements, by themselves, would have produced. Thus, for example, we say popularly that heat melts metals, turns water into steam, accelerates vegetable growth, &c., meaning thereby that the introduction of a greater amount of this element among the antecedents is followed by certain important changes in the consequents. In this sense of the word, a cause may have an indefinite number of effects. It will contribute to clearness, however, if retaining for "cause" its strictly scientific signification, we denote by the word "agent" an element capable of entering into many different combinations, and of modifying the effect which the remaining elements of the complex antecedent would have produced.

These principles show conclusively, that our knowledge even of the commonest natural agents must be in general very imperfect. The number of combinations, in which the effects produced by such agents have been actually examined, is usually very small compared with the number of those into which these agents are capable of entering; nor have we any general rules by means of which we can predict the operation of an agent in an untried combination. No chemist would undertake to predict the effect of the introduction of a substance into a new combination.

If, then, the phrases "unknowable," "inscrutable," and the like, be intended to denote that which cannot be *perfectly* known, every natural agent is probably unknowable. Light—heat—agents the most common, and the most carefully studied, cannot be perfectly known till we have either attained the power of predicting their action, or have examined every combination into which they can enter, and determined their effect in

Attributes of the Deity. 113

all. We have probably no right to call anything *impossible*, but no task would seem to merit this epithet more nearly. The number of possible chemical combinations, for example, *may* be infinite; the facts of organic chemistry do not, certainly, suggest a limit. Even if the number be really finite, we are still very far removed from complete knowledge. Whether, therefore, such agents be essentially unknowable or not, they are, in this sense of the term, unknowable by us now and for a long time to come.

But there is another consideration which renders it at least possible that everything may, in this sense, be unknowable by us. Our knowledge of all external things is derived through six inlets which we call the senses. We can know an external object only as it affects the senses, directly or indirectly. To each of these senses correspond one or more *qualities*, as we call them, of the objects, made known to us by that sense, and unknowable, even inconceivable, without its aid. Colour, reflective power, transparency—these qualities of bodies one born blind cannot know, nor even conceive. To such a person every part of the external world is, in our present sense of the word, unknowable. May it not be so with us all? May there not exist beings possessed of senses other than ours? If there be such, analogy would lead us to suppose that each of these additional senses would give to those who possess them knowledge of material qualities as completely unknowable by us, as colour or transparency by one born blind.

If, therefore, by "unknowable" be meant that which cannot be perfectly known, all things are unknowable. But if by the phrases "unknowable," "inscrutable," be meant that which cannot be known at all, no agent is unknowable of whose action we know, or can know, even a single effect.

Now, it is only when an agent is unknowable in the second sense of the word, that we should be justified in stigmatizing as unphilosophic the attempt to inquire into its action. It is plain that this case could never occur. For, if an agent were unknowable in this sense of the word, we could not know even its existence, and inquiry would be no less impossible than knowledge.

We have, as I have said, no general rule enabling us to predict the operations of an agent in a new combination. Yet the attainment of this power of prediction is the proper aim of Science. It is this, in fact, which is implied in the idea of Law. The establishment of a law enables us to predict the operation of an agent in a combination analogous to, but not identical with, one in which the experiment has been already made. The same idea is often expressed by the phrase "quality" or "property" of a substance. Thus, when it is said that an alkali possesses the property of combining with an acid, we mean not only to assert that it has been found so to combine in every case in which the experiment has been made, but to *predict* that if it be brought into the chemical presence of a newly-discovered acid, the result will be the same.

So also with regard to the actions of an intelligent being. We study them, not simply for the purpose of recording what men *have* done, but that we may be enabled to predict with a certain amount of probability what men *will* do under similar circumstances. In our ordinary language, we say that we study human actions in order to learn human nature. The idea is the same. It is by knowledge of human nature that we are enabled to predict human actions.

Now, the knowledge thus obtained is necessarily very imperfect. We know but incompletely even the physical part of the antecedents to a human action, and of the mental part we know scarcely anything. The inference of the nature of man, and yet more, the inference of the nature of any individual man, from the knowledge which we possess of his actions, must therefore always be uncertain. In one sense of the word, human nature, and more especially individual human nature, is "unknowable" by us. Yet no one would stigmatize as unphilosophic the attempt to acquire this necessarily imperfect knowledge. On the contrary, it is an attempt which we expect every historian to make. We expect that he will endeavour to appreciate the character of the man or the nation whose history he writes; and if he fail to do this, we consider him to be unworthy of the name "historian." He is an annalist, but he is no more.

These are the principles which guide our inquiries, whether their subject be purely physical phenomena or the actions of finite beings. We do not admit that either substances or men are unfit subjects of inquiry, because they are probably in much "unknowable" by us; and in each case we place before our minds, as the highest purpose of such inquiry, the knowledge of the properties, or character, or "attributes" of these things or persons, so that we may be able to anticipate the effect of their presence in a hitherto untried combination. Is there any reason why an inquiry into the character of God should be governed by different principles? Ought that inquiry to be forbidden as unphilosophic, or ought its scope to be altogether different? Shall we say that true philosophy, while it requires the historian or the psychologist to investigate the attributes of man, forbids the theologian to investigate the attributes of God?

If we view this question from the stand-point of practical Theism, the answer must be as given in the text. Without some conception of the Divine attributes, practical Theism would be impossible. We could not worship an unknown and unimagined God. If, then, practical Theism be a duty, some inquiry into the attributes of God is a necessity. But my present purpose requires me rather to view the question from the stand-point of Mr. Spencer, and I do not, therefore, here assume the truth of any form of Theism more definite than that which he has indicated.

Let us assume, then, no more than this, that the causes which we see at work in nature are not *all*, but that there is behind them a mighty and mysterious Power, manifested to us in the phenomena of which it is the ultimate cause, and let us give to this Power the name of God. The existence of such a Power Mr. Spencer is prepared to recognise, and he thinks that Science must recognise it too, if she would effect a reconciliation between herself and Religion. But he adds that Religion is equally bound to admit that the mystery is absolute, and therefore to renounce all inquiry into the "attributes" of a Power which is essentially unknowable by man. The question which we have to consider is—Ought Religion to assent to this renunciation?

That man's knowledge of such a Power as that which is here indicated must be very imperfect, is evident. We have seen that this imperfection attaches to our knowledge of every natural agent; much more must it attach to our knowledge of such an agent as this. But we have seen also that it is not imperfection but impossibility of knowledge which renders inquiry unphilosophic. All our knowledge is necessarily imperfect, and if we renounce inquiry because it can only give us imperfect knowledge, we condemn ourselves to total ignorance on every subject. If, then, we would give a just answer to the question, whether the attributes of the Great First Cause be a proper subject for human inquiry, we must consider, not whether they can be perfectly known, but whether they can be known at all. The principles already laid down enable us to answer this question. No cause can be said to be wholly unknown of which we know any of the effects, and this is no less true of the Great First Cause than of any other. If it be true that behind all the causes which we see around us there exists a First Cause, of which these secondary causes are themselves effects, every effect of these causes gives us information with respect to the First Cause. Every phenomenon which we observe teaches us something of that which is the ultimate cause of all phenomena. The knowledge which we gain from any such phenomenon, or from them all combined, is small indeed compared with that which remains unknown, but it is real as far as it goes. It does not seem just, then, to condemn as unphilosophic all inquiry into the Divine attributes on the ground that the Being who is the subject of such inquiry is unknowable.

Neither may we pass such a sentence on inquiry into certain Divine attributes, because certain others are not only unknowable but unthinkable. Whether the operations of the Great First Cause are in any degree affected by human sorrow or by human prayer is a legitimate subject of inquiry, even though it be true—as it assuredly is—that infinity is essentially unthinkable.

Nay, the results which flow from a certain attribute may properly be inquired into, with the purpose of testing their reality, even though the attribute itself be unthinkable. We cannot, by any effort, picture to our minds an Omnipresent Being, but the result of the Divine Omnipresence, namely, that man's prayers are always *heard*, is perfectly intelligible.

On the whole, then, I cannot think that we should be justified in rejecting inquiry into the Divine attributes as unphilosophic, either on the ground that they are unknowable, or on the ground that some of them are unthinkable. To render the first objection true in fact, the word "unknowable" must be taken to denote imperfection, not total absence, of possible knowledge, and in this sense the objection lies against inquiry into any natural agent. The second objection lies only against inquiry into the particular attributes which are unthinkable (as

Appendix.—Attributes of the Deity.

for example, infinity), and does not always, even in such a case, forbid inquiry into the results which may follow from the existence of these attributes in the First Cause. We have now to ask—What useful purpose is served by inquiry into the attributes of the First Cause? Granting that such inquiry is not in itself unphilosophic, have we a sufficient reason for making it? To this it may, I think, fairly be replied, that the words "First Cause" are a sufficient answer to the question. When we have admitted that everything in Nature, ourselves and our own powers included, is ultimately due to the working of One Great Agent, we have surely admitted enough to invest that agent, whatever it may be, with the deepest interest for us.

Has the operation of the First Cause ceased with the establishment of a number of secondary causes, or does its activity still continue? That is our first question. If we have reason to think that the First Cause is still active, the next question presents itself irresistibly—How does it work? What do we learn from the nature of these effects, which we have agreed to ascribe to it? If all the secondary causes which are at work around us be due to the working of One First Cause, does the nature of these secondary causes teach us to look upon their Great Original as a physical force, or as an intelligent being? If the latter supposition appear to be the more probable, what analogy would seem to exist between Him and other intelligent beings of whom we have experience? *Some* analogy we must have already observed. Some perceived analogy it must have been which led us to identify the First Cause with an intelligent being. But how far do such analogies extend? How far is it true that the actions of the First Cause, which we have thus personified, are prompted by motives similar to those which govern the actions of men? Is He benevolent, merciful, just? In a word—what are His attributes? And—not less important—has man any power of modifying His actions?

All these questions are suggested so irresistibly by the recognition of a First Cause, and follow each other so naturally, that it seems difficult to understand how the human mind can forego the attempt to find some answer to each of them. It is an attempt which may wholly fail, and which can give us at best but imperfect information; but I cannot think it just to condemn as unphilosophic or unimportant an inquiry which has for its object the properties, or (to use the theological phrase) the "attributes" of the First Cause of all things.

It remains to consider, how the religious sentiment would be affected by a renunciation of all attempt to inquire into the nature of the First Cause. Suppose it to be admitted that the First Cause is, in its nature, wholly unknowable by us; suppose, for example, that we had formed no opinion upon the question, whether this Cause be an intelligent being or a physical force; what kind of religious sentiment could the mind entertain with such a conception, or rather absence of conception, of the object to which religious sentiment is directed? Not that, certainly, to which Theists, in the ordinary sense of that word, give the name. The religious sentiment, as Theists usually understand the expression, is a mixed feeling, whose constituent parts are awe and love. The second of these emotions can be evoked only by a *person*, not by a *force* or aggregate of forces. If, then, we exclude the element of personality from our conception of the First Cause, we necessarily deprive the religious sentiment of the element of love. Even if the element of personality were not excluded, the religious sentiment would still be devoid of the element of love, unless man had formed some conception of the moral attributes of the First Cause. The religious sentiment being thus deprived of the element of love, what would remain? What sentiment would be excited in the human mind by the conviction that, above and beyond all that we see, there exists a tremendous Power, the ultimate cause of all phenomena, but in its own nature unknown and unknowable; an inscrutable mystery which we must not even seek to penetrate? Doubtless there *is* such a sentiment. A mysterious Power, of which we know nothing but some terrible effect, does awaken in our hearts a very deep and real feeling, simply because it *is* mysterious. When an epidemic sweeps over a village and destroys half of its inhabitants, the feeling which such a calamity awakens is all the more intense, when we can point to no physical cause which might seem to have marked for destruction that village above all others; and the intensity of the feeling is lessened when we have discovered such a cause. "The pestilence that walketh in darkness" loses half its terrors, when its path has been revealed to the eye of medical science.

But while we may not doubt the reality and depth of the sentiment excited in our minds by a pestilence or any other mysterious agent of destruction, we may fairly question the propriety of calling it a *religious* sentiment. It is simply that undefined feeling of awe with which we contemplate the union of the Unknown and the Terrible. If we give to this feeling the name "religious," we are certainly using that word in a sense altogether different from its ordinary sense. It will be sufficient to indicate one essential difference. The religious sentiment, as we usually understand the expression, is distinctly moral. It is not a mere passive impression, but has a powerful influence upon man's life and actions. But the indefinite feeling of awe, which is produced by the contemplation of vast results of an unknown cause, has not this character. Only so far as the cause is known is any practical effect produced by its contemplation; and just in proportion as the effect becomes practical does the undefined awe of which I have spoken pass away. When it is said, therefore, that the religious sentiment would be exalted by substituting, as the object of man's contemplation, the idea of an unknown and unknowable cause for the Theist's conception of God, it may be fairly replied that the religious sentiment, as Theists understand the expression, is, not exalted, but wholly taken away, another and quite different feeling being substituted for it. Whether this latter be the more exalted feeling, is a question which I do not propose to discuss. But it could not, surely, in any proper sense of the words, be said to take the place of the religious sentiment as Theists understand it. It could not fulfil the purposes which the religious sentiment may and does fulfil. Love of God—the religious sentiment of the Theist—is a feeling eminently practical. He who regards with a mingled feeling of affection and awe a Being whom he believes to love virtue and to abhor vice will find in *that* religious sentiment a powerful incentive to the one and a powerful deterrent from the other. But no man will live a purer or a nobler life, because he believes in the existence of an inscrutable Cause, of whose nature he has not formed any conception, not even attempting to decide the question, whether this Great Cause is to be regarded as an impersonal force, or as a sentient being.

On the whole, then, I do not think that we are justified in regarding the First Cause as absolutely unknowable, nor that, if such a conclusion were justified, the religious sentiment would be changed for the better. If these conclusions be true, we have no right to condemn, as unphilosophic or useless, the theologian's attempt to inquire into the attributes of God. I may remark that no inquiry which man can make could deprive his Theistic sentiments of that element of awe which is excited by the presence of the unknown. That which we know of God must always bear so small a proportion to that which we do not know, that this element can never be obliterated.

NOTE D, PAGE 15.

ULTIMATE CRITERION OF TRUTH.

The criterion of Truth has been the subject of a protracted controversy between Mr. Mill and Mr. Herbert Spencer. I do not purpose to enter upon this controversy, which will be found in Mill's *System of Logic*, Book II., chap. 7; and in Spencer's *Principles of Psychology*, vol. II., part vii., chap. 11.

The criterion as I have stated it, following Mr. Goldwin Smith, nearly agrees with the conclusions of Mr. Spencer, with, however, a certain difference which I shall point out further on. For the present I wish to consider the question itself— What is the criterion of truth? Before we can answer this question, we must consider what meaning we attach to the words "criterion of truth." Now, it is plain that we have, and can have, no means of distinguishing between that which *is* true, and that which we *believe* to be true, unless the word "believe" be understood to include in its signification a certain amount of doubt. We do indeed frequently use a form of words which appears to convey some such distinction. We say that we *believe* a statement to be true, but that we do not *know* it to be true. In this case, however, it is plain that the mental attitude, which we denote by the word "believe," is not free from doubt. Sometimes, too, the word "know" is applied to conviction produced by a particular kind of evidence, namely, personal observation. But if these special meanings be set aside, that which we *believe* to be true, that which we *know* to be true, and that which *is* true, are for us one and the same thing. To believe a statement to be true and to know it to be true are, if doubt be excluded, only different forms of expression for the same mental phenomenon; and that which we know or believe to be true is wholly undistinguishable by us from that which is true. The power of commanding undoubting belief forms the essential difference of a class of statements which we have no means of distinguishing from truth. Belief is a mental phenomenon which, by an irresistible necessity of our nature, we are obliged to refer to an external cause, namely, objective truth. Only by the presence of the internal phenomenon do we know the existence of the external cause, and whenever the internal phenomenon exists, we are compelled to infer the existence of the external cause. In this sense, therefore, undoubting belief is a *criterion* of truth. In fact, belief includes the reference of the internal phenomenon to the external cause.

It may be said that this reference is frequently erroneous, and that the internal phenomenon often results from a cause different from the supposed external cause. This is certainly true; but the legitimate inference from this want of constant correspondence is simply, that man has no unerring rule for the attainment of truth. Objective truth is a cause which we can know only by its effect on our own minds. If that effect be belief, we recognise the existence of this particular cause, for belief implies this recognition. If the effect which we call belief be not produced, the cause, objective truth, whether present or not, is for us as though it did not exist. The cause, truth, does not always produce the effect, belief; and the effect, belief, is frequently produced by causes different from truth; but it is certain that the cause can be known to us only by the effect; and the fact, that the connexion between these two is not invariable, is only another statement of the fact, that man has no unerring means of arriving at objective truth. There is for us no other truth than *that which commands our undoubting belief.*

Admitting, however, that undoubting belief is, in this sense, our only possible criterion of truth, we may still inquire, Is there no distinction among the propositions to which we award this undoubting belief? Can we not recognise, in some of these propositions, a claim to the title of objective truth higher than that possessed by others? And if we can, may we not give the name "criterion of truth" to the distinction, whatever it be, which marks out this class from the rest? In reply to this question we may say, in the first place, that all propositions which command our undoubting belief are to each one of us, considered in their relation to objective truth, perfectly equal. Undoubting belief is but another name for certainty, and certainty does not admit of degrees. We can, then, distinguish among propositions which command our undoubting belief, only by introducing an element of doubt into the feeling with which we regard some of them, and thus removing these beliefs from the category in which they had previously stood.

This process of verifying or modifying our beliefs varies with the nature of the propositions to which it is applied. If these propositions be derived from other propositions previously admitted, we re-examine the process of derivation, and perhaps also the original propositions themselves. But our present concern is not with derived but with ultimate propositions. It is plain, as has been often remarked, that the process of derivation cannot go on indefinitely. The series, as we trace it back, must have a beginning. There must be propositions which command our belief by a power, not depending on any other propositions, but inherent in themselves. It is with such ultimate propositions that we are now concerned; and the question which we have to consider is this—Can we make any distinction among the propositions which command our undoubting belief without the intervention of any other propositions? Have we any means of verifying or modifying a belief which does not depend upon proof, but on the nature of the thing believed?

This, as we have seen, can only be done by introducing doubt into the feeling with which we regard some of these propositions. Now in every case, in which belief is really a necessity of our nature, doubt is impossible. We must, therefore, endeavour to determine, whether the belief which we accord to each of these propositions be of this kind, or whether it be due to some other cause which more careful reflection might remove. For this problem we have, as I have said in the text, no general solution. But we do very largely exclude one kind of delusive belief, by adopting as our criterion of truth, not simply belief in the proposition itself, but the impossibility of believing the contrary. The application of this criterion excludes, as I have before said, that kind of indolent assent which we sometimes give almost without thought. Ask a man whether he believes a certain proposition, and if the proposition be familiar to him, and have been accepted by those around him, he will probably reply without hesitation, and with no appearance of doubt, that he does believe it. But it is quite possible that his belief, or that which he takes for belief, may amount to no more than this—that it has never occurred to him to doubt it. The affirmative has been suggested to him, but not the negative; and the unreality of the belief is at once shown by its disappearance when the negative *is* suggested. But ask him whether it be *impossible to disbelieve* the proposition, and the question itself suggests the negative. The question suggests also, or rather demands, a mental effort, before it can be truthfully answered, and thus guards him, though not indeed perfectly, against that indolent acquiescence which is at once so common and so entirely valueless. It is for this reason that impossibility of disbelief is to be preferred, as a criterion of truth, to undoubting belief.

It may, perhaps, be objected that if the criterion of truth be undoubting belief, or something equivalent to undoubting belief, this equivalent should be rather impossibility of *un*belief than impossibility of *dis*belief. Impossibility of unbelief does no doubt imply impossibility of disbelief, but it may be contended that impossibility of disbelief does not necessarily imply impossibility of unbelief. But, although it is certainly true that unbelief does not imply disbelief, we may, I think, in the present case, use them indifferently. Impossibility of disbelief must imply either impossibility of unbelief or impossibility of arriving at *any* conclusion—absolute scepticism, in fact. But this is a state of mind with which we have here no concern. We are now considering only those propositions which the mind *believes*, for the purpose of determining whether any distinction can be made among *them*. We have therefore no concern with propositions as to which the mind is sceptical.

There is an ambiguity in the expression, impossibility of disbelief, which it may be well to notice, although, as I shall show, it does not strictly concern us here. When we say that it is impossible to disbelieve a proposition, we may mean either that the proposition is of such a kind that we cannot conceive the production of *any* evidence which would induce us to disbelieve it; or, we may mean that disbelief is impossible in the present state of the evidence as known to us. Impossibility of disbelief, in the first sense, is the best criterion of truth which we can have. Impossibility of disbelief, in the second sense, is not a criterion of truth, unless we are sure that we know all the evidence. If we only know *part*, impossibility of disbelief ought to be accepted by us not as a criterion of that which is certainly true, but only of that which is probably true, the degree of probability depending upon the completeness of our knowledge of the evidence. In the present case, where we are concerned, not with derived but with ultimate propositions, for which there is no evidence, there is no ambiguity in the expression, "impossibility of disbelief." It denotes simply, that the constitution of man's mind and the nature of the proposition are such, that he finds disbelief to be impossible.

Before proceeding further, I wish to make some remarks on the criterion of truth as defined by Mr. Spencer, which differs in some respects from that which I have here stated. Mr. Spencer[1] insists strongly on the difference between incredibility and inconceivability. The ultimate criterion of the truth of a proposition is, he thinks, not that the contradictory of the proposition is simply *incredible*, but that it is *inconceivable*.

It is necessary then to inquire—What is the difference between the ideas expressed by these words respectively? What is the difference between the assertion that a statement is inconceivable, and the assertion that it is incredible? And, in the first place—What do we mean by this latter assertion? More, certainly, than simple disbelief. We disbelieve many statements which we should not call incredible. But we call a statement incredible when we feel that it is beyond the reach of any possible evidence to convince us of its truth. Now, this incredibility may arise, either from the nature of the proposition itself, or from the evidence which we already possess on the subject. Thus the statement that two right lines inclose a space is incredible, and the statement that the Nile flows into the Red Sea is incredible; but the incredibility of the one statement is of a different kind from that of the other. In the former case the nature of the ideas compared, namely, the idea of two right lines and the idea of space-inclosing power, is such that they cannot, by any mental effort, be brought into that relation which we call agreement. In the second case, the incredibility of the statement does not arise from the nature of the ideas compared. Considered in themselves, these ideas can be brought together without difficulty in the relation of agreement. The statement is incredible because we cannot admit its truth without rejecting as untrue an enormous mass of evidence

[1] *Principles of Psychology*, vol. ii., p. 408.

by which it is shown that the Nile flows into the Mediterranean.

These two statements appear to exemplify the only logical distinction between a proposition which is inconceivable and a proposition which is simply incredible. In an inconceivable proposition the ideas compared are so completely repugnant, that no mental effort can bring them into the same mental picture. In a proposition which is simply incredible without being inconceivable, it does indeed appear to us impossible to bring the ideas into agreement; but the impossibility results, not from the repugnancy of the ideas themselves, but from the existence of *evidence* which the acceptance of the proposition would compel us to reject, although it appears to us so perfectly convincing that we cannot refuse to believe it. In such a proposition it is not impossible to bring the ideas into the same mental picture.

It must be remarked, however, that this is not an ultimate proposition. So far we have only succeeded in resolving one incredibility into another. The statement that the Nile flows into the Red Sea is incredible, not in itself, but because it is incredible that so many witnesses who have declared that the Nile flows into the Mediterranean, uncontradicted by even a single witness asserting that it flows into the Red Sea, should have spoken falsely. But why is this supposition incredible? Because, some writers would say, we have found by experience that, when a large number of witnesses testify of their own knowledge to the truth of an asserted fact, the asserted fact *is* true. This statement may have one of two meanings. It may be meant that experience *ought* to be the foundation of our belief in testimony, and that any belief not so founded is unphilosophic; or it may be meant that experience actually *is* the foundation of this belief. Taken in the latter sense, the statement is, I think, inconsistent with fact. Belief in testimony is antecedent to any such general induction as is here spoken of. As a matter of fact, we learn from experience rather distrust than confidence in testimony. Children do not begin with scepticism, advancing gradually to belief. The progress is quite in the opposite direction. But assuming the statement to be intended in the first sense of the words, and conceding that conformity to experience is the only philosophical foundation for belief in testimony—a proposition which is certainly not self-evident—the question still remains—Why is a statement incredible because it is not conformable to experience? Thus, in the present example, concurrent and uncontradicted testimony has been found to be trustworthy in a thousand cases. Why is it incredible that it should be deceptive in the thousand and first case?

To take this instance in its strongest form. A thousand witnesses have testified to the truth of each of a thousand facts of the same nature—geographical facts, for example. We have found that in every one of these cases the testimony of the witnesses was true. If the same witnesses testify to the truth of another geographical fact, not possessing any inherent improbability, and not contradicted by any witness, why do we reject as incredible the supposition that their united testimony may, in this instance, be false?

I do not think that we can push the analysis further back. We cannot, as in the former case, resolve the incredibility of the supposition into that of another supposition which is implied by the first. If this be so, it does not seem possible to give to the question just stated any answer but the following:—Human nature is so constituted, that a break in uniformity so complete as that which is implied in the supposition of the falsity of the witnesses is, to it, incredible. We have seen two phenomena, the statement of the witnesses, and the truth of the fact stated, associated a thousand times. We have never known an instance of the occurrence of the first without the presence of the other. Then, by a necessity of our nature, of which, so far as I can see, we can give no account but that it *is* a necessity of our nature, we have come to regard the connexion as indissoluble, and from the known reality of the one phenomenon to infer with certainty the reality of the other. We reject, then, as incredible, the supposition that the connexion has been, in a certain case, actually dissolved. Some might be disposed to deduce the same conclusion as a case of the general principle that "like causes produce like effects." Observation of a phenomenon has, in a thousand cases, caused the witnesses to give a true report. We believe then, that, in the thousand and first case, a like cause, namely, observation of a similar phenomenon, has produced a like effect, namely, a true report; and we reject as incredible the supposition that the effect has been wholly different. But we shall see reason to doubt that this is an ultimate principle.

We have now to inquire whether the supposition of the falsity of the witnesses be inconceivable as well as incredible. If by inconceivable be meant that of which the mind can form no picture, the falsity of the witnesses is certainly *not* inconceivable. There is no difficulty in drawing a mental picture of a habitually truthful man, or any number of habitually truthful men, speaking falsely on some one occasion—even joining in the same falsehood. The picture has not, indeed, any corresponding reality, and we know that it has none. But the same may be said of many other mental pictures. They have no corresponding reality. It is impossible to believe that they have a corresponding reality; but it is not impossible to draw the picture. It is not impossible to draw a mental picture of a red hot bar of iron standing in a barrel of gunpowder without an explosion, although it is impossible to believe that such a thing could be. In a word, it is *incredible*, but it is not *inconceivable*.

Ultimate Criterion of Truth.

But it *is* impossible to draw a mental picture of two right lines inclosing a space. The attempt to construct such a picture would show that the elements which it is attempted to combine are essentially discordant, and that no mental effort could succeed in bringing them together in the same picture. That two right lines should inclose a space is, therefore, more than incredible—it is also inconceivable.

If this be the true distinction between things inconceivable and things simply incredible, we can see why we ought to assume, as the ultimate criterion of truth, not the inconceivability of the opposite, but its incredibility. If the list of ultimate truths included those only of which the opposite is inconceivable in this sense of the word, we have already seen that we should lose one of the most important principles which we possess, namely, the principle of uniformity. With the principle of uniformity we should also lose another not less important, namely, the principle which may be called the foundation of all the scientific knowledge which we derive from experience—the principle by which an isolated fact is converted into a general truth—the principle, namely, that "like causes produce like effects."

It may perhaps be contended that the production of different effects by the *same* cause is in itself inconceivable. I do not think that this is true; but, even if it were, it would be of no importance to our present purpose. From the principle thus stated we can derive nothing. Every one of the collections of conditions which we call physical causes is unique. No two are identical. The element of time or of place varies, even if there be no other change; and the principle, as we really use it, is, that if the other conditions continue unaltered, a change in the element of time or of place causes no change in the result.

Now we can hardly say that the contradictory of this proposition is inconceivable. Indeed, prior to experience, it is not, in the strict sense of the word, incredible. There does not seem to be any absurdity in the supposition that the course of nature might have been such, that the relation between cause (in the ordinary meaning of the word) and effect might be, not fixed, but variable with the time. Or, to speak more accurately, a cosmical arrangement according to which the element of time should form an essential part of the system of antecedents which we call the cause is not inconceivable. It is not impossible to draw a mental picture of a world in which such an arrangement is the law of nature. If then the inconceivability of the contradictory be the test of an ultimate truth, the proposition (or axiom) which is the base of all physical science is not an ultimate truth. Why then should it be regarded as a truth at all? It may be said that we learn by experience that the elements of time and place do not influence the relation between cause and effect. But this is not true. All that we learn from experience is, that, in a finite number of observed cases, this relation *has* remained unchanged. That it has remained unchanged in a number of unobserved cases, or that it will *always* so remain, are wholly different propositions, which can be deduced from the observed facts only by the help of the principle stated in p. 129, namely, that a phenomenon which has been observed in a large number of cases will occur in *every* similar case. This, if it be not the principle of causation itself, is the principle of simple uniformity, of which we have seen that the contradictory is not inconceivable. The criterion adopted by Mr. Spencer, if the word "inconceivable" be understood in its proper sense, would deprive us of the principle of uniformity, and, with it, of the principle of causation.

It is necessary to observe that the sense in which I have used the word "incredible" is, if I rightly apprehend him, different from that which Mr. Spencer assigns to "unbelievable." This word, as he uses it, seems to denote no more than *difficulty* of belief, differing sensibly from *impossibility*. Mr. Spencer says—"An unbelievable proposition is one which admits of being framed in thought, but is so much at variance with experience, in which its terms have habitually been otherwise united, that its terms cannot be put in the alleged relation without effort. Thus it is unbelievable that a cannon-ball fired in England should reach America; but it is not inconceivable."[1]

I readily admit that we do not pronounce a proposition to be *certainly* true when its opposite is "unbelievable" in the sense in which Mr. Spencer here uses the word. But it seems doubtful whether this use of the word be admissible. If the mind can by any effort bring together the subject and predicate of a proposition, in the connexion which the proposition assigns to them, we should hardly call the proposition *un*believable. It is *difficult* of belief, in a degree proportional to the mental effort by which the subject and predicate are brought together, but it is not absolutely "unbelievable." Thus, we may inquire—to take the example which Mr. Spencer gives—Is it unbelievable that a cannon-ball fired in England should reach America? Now, dynamical science can calculate the velocity of projection necessary to give such a range to a cannon-ball. The question which we have to consider is therefore this—Is it unbelievable that such a velocity of projection should be given to a cannon-ball? The answer to this question must depend upon the sense in which it is understood. If the question be—Is it unbelievable that a ball discharged in England from any cannon hitherto constructed, by any means hitherto employed, should reach America? the answer must be—Yes, for it involves the supposition that two wholly different effects follow from similar causes. We can calculate the velocity which would be communicated to the cannon-ball by an expansive force, acting during the whole

[1] *Principles of Psychology*, vol. ii. p. 408.

time of the ball's passage through a space somewhat less than the length of the cannon, and whose intensity (to take the most favourable case) is maintained throughout at a point just below that of the bursting force. We know that the velocity so communicated, in the longest and strongest cannon which was ever cast, would be insufficient to carry the ball through the required distance. Taken in this sense, the proposition *is* unbelievable. But if the proposition be, that a cannon might be cast and an explosive substance employed, which would communicate to the ball the required velocity, such a proposition would certainly *not* be unbelievable—although, for reasons upon which it is unnecessary to enter, it would be very difficult of belief. In common language, we could not pronounce such a phenomenon to be *impossible*, but only highly *improbable*. If the signification of the word "unbelievable," as Mr. Spencer uses it, be truly indicated by the proposition which he has given, understood in this latter sense, it may readily be admitted that we ought not to receive a proposition as certainly true, because its opposite is unbelievable. But this use of the word "unbelievable" seems hardly consistent with its etymology.

There is still another objection to the acceptance of inconceivability as the criterion of truth. We may fairly ask—Is every inconceivable proposition also incredible? If we find ourselves unable to bring together in the same mental picture the ideas which are denoted by the terms of the proposition, do we therefore assume that agreement between them is impossible? Thus, for example, a merciful man may be wholly unable to picture to himself a human mind delighting in the contemplation of human suffering, regarded merely as suffering, and with no feeling of hostility to the sufferer. Ought he to consider this combination impossible? Plainly not; for there is historical evidence amply sufficient to convince him that the combination has frequently existed.

Ultimate Criterion of Truth. 135

"There have been human minds so constituted as to take pleasure in witnessing the suffering of a fellow-creature." Here we have a proposition which is, to a certain class of minds, *inconceivable*, but not *incredible*. In such a case, therefore, inconceivability, regarded as a criterion of truth, fails, and would be rejected even by the mind which had found itself unable to form the conception.

This instance indicates a class of cases in which inconceivability is necessarily an erroneous criterion of truth. The inability, felt by some minds, to conceive as true the proposition stated above, results from the inability of such minds to form a sufficiently general conception of that which is expressed by the term "mind." This is a concrete term denoting the aggregate of certain powers and qualities; and this aggregate is not conceived by all persons alike. The conception which each man forms of the human mind is derived, not wholly, but very largely, from observation of his own mind. Thus formed, the conception will naturally include qualities which are prominent in the mind by which it is formed. Some of these qualities may be so closely interwoven into the texture of the individual mind, that it may be wholly unable to conceive a mind from which these qualities are absent. Thus, in the present instance, the mind of a humane man may be unable to conceive a mind from which all kindly feelings are banished. When such a man endeavours to bring together in one picture the human mind, as he conceives it, and the quality of taking pleasure in the suffering of another, he cannot help seeing that the elements which he attempts to combine are repugnant. The picture is one which he cannot form. In other words, the proposition, in which this combination is asserted, is to him inconceivable. If therefore the inconceivability of the opposite were a test of, at least, subjective truth, the proposition—No human mind can take pleasure in the suffering of another—

would be, to such a man, certainly true. This, as we know, is not the case. The proposition is certainly false, and would be recognised as false even by the person who was incapable of embodying its contradictory in a mental picture. The inconceivability of the contradictory is not therefore in such a case a reliable criterion of subjective truth.

The same uncertainty may attend the application of this criterion in every case in which one of the terms of the proposition is concrete. If, as in the case which has just been considered, inability to conceive the truth of a proposition results from inability to form an adequate conception of that which is denoted by the concrete term, the proposition may be perfectly credible and yet inconceivable. We may be convinced by evidence that the conception we have formed is inadequate, and yet be unable to form any other conception. We may, therefore, be convinced by evidence that a proposition is true, and yet be unable to conceive it as true.

It must be remembered that, in such a case as that which has been here discussed, the inconceivability attaches solely to the mental phenomenon, not to the external acts which follow it. There is no difficulty in forming a conception of the external act of going to witness the torture of a fellow-creature. We may even conceive—although, to a man such as I have described, this is more difficult—the appearance of the external signs of pleasure. But it is when we endeavour to "account for" this phenomenon—when we try to picture to ourselves the state of mind which these signs indicate—that the task becomes to some minds impossible.

Theology furnishes many examples of such propositions. The Divine attribute of omnipresence is certainly inconceivable, or to use the modern expression, unthinkable. If, then, inconceivability were to be regarded as the criterion of falsehood, the proposition, God is omnipresent, should be regarded as false.

We know that by very many it is not so regarded. The proposition is inconceivable, but it is not incredible. In fact, it is believed by every one who prays.

On the whole, I think that we are justified in adopting as the ultimate criterion of truth, not the inconceivability, but the incredibility of the contradictory. The adoption of the former would deprive us of some undoubted truths, and would admit into the list of truths propositions which would be rejected as untrue even by the individual to whom the contradictory was inconceivable.

But, even in this form, the criterion of truth requires some explanatory observations before we can practically use it. Our field of knowledge would be very narrow if it only included propositions whose contradictories are incredible in the strict sense of that word, in which it denotes *impossibility* of belief. This, however, is not the meaning which is really attached to the word "incredible," as commonly used. If we examine carefully the statements to which we give that name, we shall find that it denotes in general no more than a very high degree of improbability. Even where the improbability is so high as not to be distinguishable by the human mind from impossibility, it is still true that the difference between the statements which we call incredible and those which we call simply improbable is very commonly a difference not in kind but in degree. The evidence against both classes of propositions is often quite the same in kind, differing only in amount. Thus, for example, there is often no generic difference between the testimony which is no more than enough to make a proposition slightly improbable, and that which is so multiplied as to make a proposition incredible. In all propositions which are established or disproved by cumulative evidence, there is no break in the series of probabilities which extends from a probability of truth so great as to be undistinguishable from certainty to a probability of falsehood so great as to be undistinguishable from incredibility.

It is for this reason that I have taken as the ultimate criterion of truth, to us, not *impossibility*, but *difficulty* of disbelief. This difficulty is capable of all degrees from a very slight difficulty, indicating a very slight probability, up to a difficulty so great as not to be distinguishable from impossibility, indicating a probability so high as not to be distinguishable from certainty. The greater part of those propositions which we call *certain* are not separated by any generic distinction from propositions which are only highly probable. Indeed, if we take into account the fallibility of the human intellect, it may reasonably be doubted whether even demonstration can give us more than a very high probability. If this be not so, it seems difficult to account for mathematical controversy—an undoubted fact in the history of science.

Are there any ultimate propositions which belong to the category of probable truths? Only one, I think; but that one is the foundation of every general truth concerning real things which we possess; it is the principle of *incomplete* uniformity. And uniformity always *is* incomplete; if it were not so, it could give us no new truth. We believe a certain thing to be true in a number of *unobserved* cases, because (to take the most favourable supposition) in all *observed* cases it has been found to be true. This statement of the principle shows that the uniformity is necessarily incomplete. For if it were complete, there *could* be no unobserved case. We can say no more than this—that the uniformity exists in all the cases which have come under our observation; and, by proposing to apply the principle to an unobserved case, we admit that all cases have not come under our observation.

Now, the assurance which we derive from such a uniformity is essentially progressive, and, as such, can never differ, in kind, from probability. The observed uniformity may be so wide—the number of observed cases may be so great—that the assurance which we obtain from the principle cannot be practically distinguished from certainty, but in its essence it is no more than a high probability. Thus, for example, if a person, of whom we only know that he had made one true statement, should make a second statement, not possessing any inherent improbability, we should in all likelihood believe him. But the belief would not be strong. A very slight amount of opposing evidence would be sufficient to change it into disbelief. If then we were asked—Do you believe that to be true which the witness asserts? we should probably reply in the affirmative. But if we were asked—Would you find it impossible to disbelieve it? we should reply, No, nor even very difficult. This difficulty, very small at first, increases with every fresh instance of truthfulness of the witness, until after the occurrence of a very large number of such instances, extending over a long period, and uninterrupted by a single instance of untruthfulness, the difficulty becomes so great as to be practically undistinguishable from impossibility. But the gradual process by which this mental attitude has been reached shows that, *in kind*, it is but *difficulty* still. *Difficulty*, therefore, not *impossibility* of disbelief, is the criterion of truth as applied to the principle of uniformity.

To avoid this conclusion some might be disposed to fall back on the idea of causation, and to consider the proposition—"Like causes produce like effects"—to be an ultimate principle. I have before given some reasons for refusing to it this title. But, waiving this point, it may readily be shown that the principle in question is, as applied to real phenomena, no more than probable. Even if it were admitted to be certain that two systems of antecedents differing only in the elements of time or place—and this is the nearest approach to identity which any two systems of antecedents can present—will have consequents identical in the same sense, we know that even this approximation to identity is not presented by any combination of real phenomena. Even in the case of an experiment, where the utmost care is taken to secure an exact reproduction of certain conditions, we know that such a reproduction is practically impossible. However carefully the experiment be conducted, absolute identity with the pattern is not to be looked for. Some variation in the antecedent, and, corresponding to this, some variation in the consequent, cannot be avoided; and the principle which we use in predicting the result of an experiment is really this—that, if we reproduce approximately the prescribed conditions, we shall produce approximately the expected result. This principle is so far from being absolutely certain, that it is known not to be universally true. In general, no doubt, experience teaches us that a small difference of antecedent produces no more than a small difference of consequent. But experience teaches us also that there are cases in which an inappreciably small difference of antecedent will produce an enormous difference of consequent. The difference between the temperature which leaves a mass of gunpowder apparently unchanged, and that which causes it to explode and spread destruction round it may be but an infinitesimal fraction of a degree. The former case is indeed very much more common, and we may therefore anticipate with a high degree of probability that effects nearly identical will follow from causes nearly identical. But to this principle there are real exceptions, which, prior to experience, we have no *general* method of determining. The principle that "Like" (as distinguished from identical) "causes produce like effects" possesses, therefore, no more than a high probability.

On the whole, then, I think it appears that the basis of all general physical knowledge is a principle which is no more than probable. Belief in the contradictory of this principle is not impossible, but only very difficult. *Difficulty* of disbelief is therefore, in this case, to us, the ultimate criterion of truth.

NOTE E, PAGE 17.

RIGHT OF THE MORAL FACULTY TO JUDGE OF THE DIVINE ATTRIBUTES.

No questions in Natural Theology have, in the present day, attracted more attention or elicited greater diversities of opinion than those which concern the right of man's moral sense to judge of the morality of actions or purposes attributed to God. Some have maintained that the right does not exist. Man, they say, when he attempts to form such a judgment, undertakes a work to which his powers are wholly unequal. The moral sense was given him to guide his own actions, not to judge of the actions of his Creator. In the pride of his heart he may indeed assume to himself such an office, but the task is too great for him. He has entered upon a path which will lead him, not to truth, but to ruinous error.

Even writers, who would refuse to pronounce so extreme a sentence, seem to discourage this kind of inquiry. Thus Mansel:—" The primary and proper employment of man's moral sense, as of his other faculties, is not *speculative*, but *regulative*. It is not designed to tell us what are the absolute and immutable principles of Right, as existing in the eternal nature of God; but to discern those relative and temporary manifestations of them, which are necessary for human training in this present life. . . . . The primary and direct inquiry which human reason is entitled to make concerning a professed revelation is, how far does it tend to promote or to hinder the moral discipline of man. It is but a secondary and indirect question, and one very liable to mislead, to ask how far it is compatible with the Infinite Goodness of God."—*Limits of Religious Thought*, pp. 157–8.

On the other hand the author (F. W. Newman), from whom Mansel quotes, and against whom the foregoing passage is directed, would give to the moral sense the absolute right of deciding on this compatibility.

"The human mind is competent to sit in *moral* and *spiritual* judgment on a professed revelation, and to decide, if the case seem to require it, in the following tone :—This doctrine attributes to God that which we should call harsh, cruel, or unjust in man: it is, therefore, essentially inadmissible."—F. W. Newman, *The Soul*, p. 58.

"With respect to the moral treatment of His creatures by Almighty God, all men, in different degrees, are able to be judges of the representations made of it, by reason of the moral sense which He has given them."—H. B. Wilson in *Essays and Reviews*, p. 153.

In reply to the first class of opinions, it may fairly be asked— By what authority do we deny to the moral sense, or any other human faculty, the right to judge of *any* question which comes before it ? *Primâ facie* each faculty has this right, and he who, in any particular case, denies it, is bound to justify the denial. If he cannot do this, the faculty retains its natural right to judge of everything of which it *can* judge.

Thus when Mansel denies the right of the moral sense to judge of "the absolute and immutable principles of right, as existing in the eternal nature of God," it is for him to *dis*prove it, not for the assertor of the right to prove it. He says that the moral sense was not designed to tell us what these principles are. But how is this negative to be proved ? How are we to ascertain what things the moral sense was *not* designed to tell us ? There are no doubt certain things which are not within its cognizance. It can give no information on subjects which belong to the province of pure intellect. It takes no note of the relations of geometry. It tells us nothing of the phenomena of matter. But it does take cognizance of a certain quality of voluntary actions, and it professes to extend this cognizance to the voluntary actions of *all* agents. It knows no limitation to the principles which it has established. They are, for it, the absolute and immutable principles of right, applicable to *all* cases. The disposition which is ready to make a sacrifice for the welfare of another is, so far, morally good; the disposition which takes pleasure in the pain of another is, so far, morally bad, in whatever beings these dispositions respectively exist. I cannot see, therefore, that an action has a right to claim exemption from the judgment of the moral sense, because this action is ascribed to God. I have shown in the text that this exemption, if consistently carried out, would leave no logical standing ground to Revealed Religion.

Suppose, for example, that it was stated, in a document claiming to be inspired, that God had once given to man an untrue revelation. Suppose that the claim of this document to inspiration was supported by external proofs possessing a certain amount of force. Should we be justified in bringing this supposed revelation under the judgment of the moral faculty, and rejecting it, because that faculty decided that the action attributed to God was immoral? If this question be answered in the negative, the retort is obvious—Why do you believe the Word of God at all? If your moral faculty can tell you no more than this, that untruthfulness is immoral *in man*, how do you know that truthfulness is an attribute of God? If you do not know that truthfulness is an attribute of God, of what value is Revelation?

On the other hand, if the question be answered in the affirmative—if we *do* trust our moral sense, when it tells us of the truthfulness of God, the retort is equally obvious—By what right do you single out one Divine attribute from the rest—conceding to the moral faculty the right to judge of that one—denying to the same faculty the right to judge of any of the others? If the moral faculty may decide that a certain quality, *as man understands it*, is essential to the perfect nature of God, why is its decision to be limited to a single attribute? If we concede to our moral faculty the right to reject a doctrine which would represent God as untruthful, why should we deny to it the right to reject a doctrine which would represent Him as unjust, selfish, or cruel? If justice, benevolence, and mercy, as existing in God, are to be understood to denote qualities substantially different from those which we call by the same names, as existing in man, may not the same rule be applicable to truthfulness also? If this be so, the epithet, God of Truth, becomes, to us, unmeaning, and the foundation of Revealed Religion is taken away. This seems to be the necessary result of a theory which denies to the moral faculty the right to judge of the morality of actions attributed to God.

"If God may be (what we should call) *cruel*, He may equally well be (what we should call) *a liar;* and if so, of what use is His word to us?"[1]

On the other hand, it seems difficult to admit the claim of the moral sense to an absolute supremacy. Thus, for example, let it be supposed that proofs are laid before the intellect sufficient to convince it that a certain doctrine comes from God. Suppose also that the moral sense condemns this doctrine as immoral. Are we justified in pronouncing that the decision of the moral sense is necessarily right? I think not. The moral sense is not infallible—no human faculty is so. Moreover, the decisions of the moral sense are given with very different de-

[1] F. W. Newman, *The Soul*, pp. 58-9.

grees of assurance. In some cases it pronounces with perfect certainty—in others it gives but a hesitating verdict. We have surely no right to declare that a decision of the moral sense, however hesitating, ought to prevail against a decision of the intellect, however assured. It is therefore possible that the proofs of the Divine origin of a doctrine may be sufficient to outweigh an objection coming from the moral sense, compelling us to adopt the conclusion that in this case the intellect was right and the moral sense wrong. But, as I have said in the text, I believe this to be a rare case. The task imposed on the intellect in deciding such a question is so complex, as compared with the simple intuition of the moral sense, that it must necessarily afford more room for the intervention of error. If then the opposition be between a process of reasoning and a simple moral intuition, I think that we are bound to decide in favour of the latter.

But we must be careful, in the application of this principle, that the evidence to which we thus give the preference *is* that of a simple intuition. For it is quite true that the judgment of the moral sense is often wrong; not because the intuition itself is wrong, but because the judgment has been pronounced upon an erroneous or imperfect statement of the facts of the case. For this error the intellect, not the moral sense, is responsible, the statement of facts being the office of the intellect. If then, under such circumstances, we give a preference to the evidence afforded by a moral judgment over the evidence afforded by a supposed revelation, we may be in reality preferring, not a moral intuition to an intellectual process, but one intellectual process to another.

This caution is especially necessary when we attempt to decide on the morality, not of an abstract quality, but of a concrete action. In this case, a large part of the process is intellectual. It is the intellect which must collect and put together the facts on which, in such a case, the moral judgment is founded. Not unfrequently too, if the ascertained facts be too few to define the action sufficiently for the formation of a moral judgment, the intellect attempts to supply the deficiency by hypothesis. Then the decision of the moral faculty is given, not on the real case, which is but imperfectly known, but on a case which has been artificially completed by the assumption of additional facts or motives. The decision itself is probably right; but it has been given on an imaginary case, and is therefore worthless; unless indeed, as sometimes happens, the imaginary case is made to assume the character of a doctrine.

A remarkable instance of a moral decision of this kind is to be found in the history of the Calvinistic controversy. The strongest argument againstt he supra-lapsarian doctrine of reprobation is derived from its repugnancy to man's moral nature. It is contended that this doctrine is condemned by the conscience as immoral, and therefore inconsistent with the attributes of God. To this it is sometimes replied[1] that the same objection lies against the permission of the existence of evil, where no Theist would admit its validity. But this is not true. The doctrine of reprobation is more than a statement—it is a theory of the existence of evil. It supplements the undoubted facts by the suggestion of a *motive*. God has permitted the existence of evil; nay more, He has created evil men, in order that their eternal punishment may augment His own glory. Now, it is plain that the addition of this motive renders the question which is submitted to the moral faculty much more definite, and thus gives to its judgment much greater weight. In truth, it substitutes a question which the moral faculty is competent to decide for one which is beyond its reach. To decide that

---

[1] Whately—*Difficulties in the Writings of St. Paul*, p. 145.

the permission of the existence of evil is inconsistent with the character of a just and merciful God, the moral faculty must be satisfied that no possible motive could justify this permission. To decide that the doctrine of reprobation is inconsistent with the character of a just and merciful God, it is only necessary that the moral faculty should be satisfied that the creation of evil would not be justified by the motive which this doctrine assigns to Him. The former decision is one which, I conceive, the moral faculty has no right to make: not because it is incapable of forming an idea of justice and mercy as they exist in God, but because the circumstances, the nature of the connexion between the evil which is in the world and the Creator of the world, and the purposes which evil may be intended to serve, are so imperfectly known to us, that the moral faculty has not the elements upon which it could properly found a decision. The case presented to it by the intellect is not sufficiently definite. It is quite otherwise with the second decision. The question which is there proposed to the moral faculty, namely—Is it consistent with the character of a just and merciful Being to bring into existence a mass of hopeless misery *with a selfish motive?*—is perfectly definite; and the right of the moral faculty to judge of it cannot be denied without excluding from the cognizance of this faculty all moral qualities, as they exist in God. Such an exclusion would leave us without any religion, Natural or Revealed.

It is often alleged, in support of the concession of supreme authority to supposed declarations of Scripture, that this concession is justified—nay, demanded—by a belief in the inspiration of the Bible. He who believes, it is said, that the Bible comes from God ought to award to Scriptural declarations, as compared with any other evidence, that supremacy which attaches to the Word of God, as compared with the word of man.

In reply to this argument, it may be observed, in the first

place, that the process of reasoning by which the inspiration of Scripture is proved is a human process, founded on evidence collected by the human intellect, and weighed by the human intellect. It does not enjoy any exemption from the errors to which every process of human reasoning is liable; and this possibility of error affects every argument derived from Scripture itself. The evidence *of* Scripture cannot be stronger than the evidence *for* Scripture. The same possibility of error attaches to the equally human processes of translation and interpretation. Supreme authority cannot, then, be fairly claimed for Scriptural arguments on the ground that the Word of God is infallible. The Word of God is indeed infallible; but there is no infallibility in the process by which the Bible is proved to *be* the Word of God. And it needs but a slight acquaintance with the works of Biblical commentators to teach us that there is no infallibility in the process by which the meaning of the Bible is ascertained.

There can be no doubt that theological, or any other, investigations would be greatly facilitated by awarding supremacy to one *kind* of evidence. Such a concession would in fact obviate the necessity of examining any but the favoured kind, unless it should happen to be silent; and, by thus simplifying our inquiries, relieve us of the perplexing doubt, which so often follows the investigation of opposing evidence. But, attractive as it is, this simplification can rarely be justified by reason. No one *kind* of evidence is so completely superior to the rest, that it ought, in all cases of conflict, to be preferred. Some writers, as we have seen, accord this supremacy to the moral sense—others to a supposed revelation; but neither verdict is consistent with reason. Indeed the very attractiveness of this simplifying process ought to excite in our minds, if not suspicion, at least caution, in accepting it. Doubt, in questions of practical importance, is so painful to the human mind, that it is happy to seize upon any method of removing it, often with very insufficient scrutiny of the principles on which the method rests. Methods of deciding which, had the voice of reason been listened to, would never have been accepted, grew into favour because they promised a decision. It was this which gave their popularity to omens and oracles—to wizards and astrology. It is this which has at least aided in procuring a ready admission of the authority of an infallible church or an infallible preacher. Impatience of doubt—unwillingness to undergo the labour necessary for its removal by the slow methods of reason—this is a frequent combination of qualities; and a process which ministers to both ought, even for that reason, to be received with grave caution. In the present instance I have endeavoured to show that it ought not to be received at all.

Before leaving this subject, I must notice a class of cases called by Mr. Mansel "Moral Miracles," in which, if his definition be right, the decision of the unaided moral faculty would be erroneous. As the question is important, I quote his own words:

"There is indeed an obvious analogy between these temporary suspensions of the laws of moral obligation and that corresponding suspension of the laws of natural phenomena which constitutes our ordinary conception of a miracle—so much so, indeed, that the former might without impropriety be designated as *Moral Miracles*. In both, the Almighty is regarded as suspending, for special purposes, not the eternal laws which constitute His own absolute nature, but the created laws which He imposed at a certain time upon a particular portion of His creatures."—*Limits of Religious Thought*, p. 159.

If in such cases the law of moral obligation be suspended, it is plain that the decision of the moral faculty, which is in conformity with this law, must be erroneous. It is therefore important to inquire—Is the moral law suspended in such cases?

The second branch of this analogy has been considered elsewhere. I have endeavoured to show (pp. 55-8) that a miracle is not a suspension of any law of Nature. Neither do I think that the cases which Mr. Mansel calls "moral miracles" can justly be regarded as suspensions of the law of moral obligation. The exceptional character of both classes of phenomena results, not from the suspension of any law, physical or moral, but from the introduction of a new element into the system of antecedents. In the physical phenomenon, the introduced element is the Divine volition. In the moral phenomenon, the introduced element is the Divine command. In both cases, the introduced element so changes the system of antecedents, that the consequent is wholly altered, yet without the suspension of a physical law in the one case, or of a moral law in the other.

This principle is plainly implied in the passage which Mr. Mansel quotes from Bishop Butler:—"There are some particular precepts in Scripture," the Bishop says, " given to particular persons, requiring actions which would be immoral and vicious, were it not for such precepts. But it is easy to see, that all these are of such a kind, as that the precept changes the whole nature of the case and of the action; and both constitutes and shows that not to be unjust or immoral, which, prior to the precept, must have appeared, and really have been so, which may well be, since *none of these precepts is contrary to immutable morality.*"—(*Analogy*, Part II., Chap. 3). This passage does not describe the suspension of moral law. On the contrary, it is plainly stated, in the sentence which I have italicised, that moral law is *not* suspended. But it is stated also that the intervention of the Divine command so changes the conditions of the action, that, although immoral if done unbidden, it becomes perfectly consistent with moral law, when done under the authority of God. This is a principle which is fully recognised in the matters of this world. An act done by authority of the

State may be perfectly moral, which done without such authority would be a heinous crime; not because the moral law which forbids the action in the second case is in the former case violated, but because it is inapplicable. Deliberately to kill an unresisting man is murder if done by a private person. Done by a public executioner, it is no crime at all. If the moral law were so stated as to include the second case—if, for example, it were declared, without reservation, criminal to kill an unresisting person—the statement would be plainly untrue. Nay, in the case mentioned, even when the sentence is unrighteous, no fault is supposed to attach to the executioner.

The assertion that a moral law is suspended means, if rightly understood, no less than this—that an action which is at one time vicious becomes at another time virtuous, without any change in the circumstances or in the motive. This is hardly even conceivable. That a change in the circumstances and in the motive should change the moral quality of the action implies no suspension of the moral law; and cases in which a moral law is supposed to have been suspended are usually of this kind.

If indeed moral distinctions were not founded in the nature of things, but owed their existence solely to the will of a superior, there would be no difficulty in imagining moral law to be suspended. But such a theory would remove the foundation of all religion.

The independent authority of the moral faculty is very distinctly stated by a late eminent writer. "By separating," says Whewell, speaking of Warburton and his school, "the idea of Obligation from that of Natural Morality, and by transferring it entirely to the Divine commands and promises, natural morality was deprived of its peculiar instruction, and incapacitated from bearing the testimony which it so readily and emphatically renders, when it is allowed to speak freely, to the perfections of God's character and the holiness of His law."

Again—"We believe our Divine Ruler to be supremely holy, just, and good; and therefore we obey Him with joy and love, as well as hope. But this distinction necessarily implies that we can form an idea of moral goodness, justice, holiness, quite other than obedience to the will of a superior."[1]

The same principle is thus expressed by Dugald Stewart:—

"If moral distinctions be not immutable and eternal, it is absurd to speak of the *goodness* or of the *justice* of God. 'Whoever thinks,' says Shaftesbury, 'that there is a God, and pretends formally to believe that He is *just* and *good*, must suppose that there is independently such a thing as *justice* and *injustice*, *truth* and *falsehood*, *right* and *wrong*, according to which eternal and immutable standards he pronounces that God is *just*, *righteous*, and *true*. If the mere will, decree, or law of God, be said absolutely to constitute *right* and *wrong*, then are these latter words of no significance at all.'"[2]

It is true, as these eminent writers have said, that if there be no morality independent of the will of God, the assertion that God is just or righteous is absolutely unmeaning. It is no less true that if the moral faculty can tell us nothing of these qualities *as they exist in God*, the assertion that God is just or righteous is quite as unmeaning in the mouth of a human being.

NOTE F, PAGE 23.

OBJECTIONS TO PRAYER DERIVED FROM THE REGULAR SEQUENCE OF PHENOMENA.

"Prayer has come into contact with scientific discovery, and I express the problem in theological terms when I say that the

[1] *History of the Moral Sciences*, pp. 129, 133, 134.
[2] *Stewart's Works*, vol. vi., p. 229 (Sir W. Hamilton's edition).

the Regular Sequence of Phenomena. 153

unchangeability of God as Lord of the physical world is expressed in modern science by the law of the conservation of force, and that that law denies the power of prayer to alter any natural sequence. . . . .

"If the doctrine of the conservation of force be true, when we pray for the fall of a single shower of five minutes in length, or the change of the direction of the wind by a single point, or the evaporation of the faintest waft of cloud, by the independent will of God, we are asking for a miracle, and for as real and tremendous a disturbance of natural law as if we had asked the postponement of the rising of the sun, or the sudden removal of the moon from the sky. There is nothing little, or nothing great, in the motion of the universe. The demand for the creation of the smallest wave of new force is as serious a demand as that for the creation of a force equivalent to that which builds up a volcano in a night."—Stopford Brooke, *Christ in Modern Life*, pp. 133–4.

I have transcribed this long passage because it states very clearly the popular objection to prayer derived from the persistency of Natural Law, giving to that objection a more than ordinary definiteness, by pointing out *the* natural law which is said to be violated by the supposed success of prayer for a physical benefit. It is, Mr. Brooke says, *the law of the conservation of force*. A shower of rain, granted in answer to human prayer, would violate this law. In fact, if I understand Mr. Brooke rightly, he thinks that the direct interference of the Divine volition in a physical sequence implies the creation of force. Is this true?

It is certainly *not* true of the interference of human volition. Man, in the exercise of his free will, can and does interfere every moment in physical sequences, wholly changing the results which would, without such interference, have followed. But we know that this change is effected without any creation of force. Thus, for example, when the exertion of man's will determines the motion of his arm, the total *amount* of force existing in the world remains unchanged. Only the distribution is affected. The exertion of man's will determines the conversion of a certain quantity of that kind of motion which we call heat into that other kind which we more usually call motion. No creation of force is involved in this conversion, by which, however, the sequence of physical phenomena may be altogether changed.

Now, I do not mean to consider the question whether, in the case of Divine interference, a creation of force may or may not take place. But assuredly, the assumption that it *does* take place is wholly unnecessary. The analogy of man's interference shows conclusively that God may intervene in a series of physical phenomena so as to change it completely, without any creation of force.

Again Mr. Brooke says:—

"The amount of rain which fell last week in England is to the millionth of an inch the exact result of a series of antecedents which not only took place some time ago about the equator and the pole, but which go back to the very beginning of things."—p. 135.

If I rightly understand this passage, and those which immediately precede it, Mr. Brooke does not include, in the series of antecedents which cause rain, the voluntary actions of men. If this be so, the statement is not true. It was said long since by Arago, in discussing the question whether Science would ever be able to predict the weather, that such prediction was in the highest degree improbable, *because* (among other reasons) the weather is in part the result of man's actions.[1] The amount of rain which fell last week in England is not the exact result of

---

[1] *Annuaire for* 1846, p. 590.

such antecedents as Mr. Brooke describes. It depends also upon the actions of the men who cut down the forests and drained the swamps.

It is true that hitherto the actions of men have produced upon the rainfall of a country only a gradual and distant effect. But no cautious thinker will pronounce a more immediate power of influencing this phenomenon to be absolutely beyond the reach of Science. If a theory of such more immediate influence were started, it would certainly be received with great scepticism. The evidence offered in support of such a theory would be subjected to a very severe scrutiny. But I do not think that any scientific man would, without examining the evidence or even the theory itself, reject it as necessarily untrue, *because* it required a creation of force. The *creation* of force is probably beyond the power of man; but we are as yet very far indeed from being able to see the limits of that which may be effected by its redistribution.

Now if we may not condemn, *as contrary to natural law*, the supposition that man may produce such an effect, still less are we warranted in pronouncing such a sentence upon the interference of God. The only principle having any claim to the title Natural Law, which may seem to be violated by the ascription of such effect to the Divine interference, is that stated in the text. We do certainly ascribe to God a power differing in kind from any power possessed by man, when we suppose that, in the case of His interference, a volition is followed by an immediate external result. This immediate sequence is indeed forbidden by the law which controls the actions of man. But the extension of such a law to the actions of God could have, as I have shown, no result but practical Atheism.

NOTE G, PAGE 25.

IS AN EMOTION A MORAL DEFECT?

The answer given to this question by the Stoical philosophy is well known. The description in the text of an emotionless man—of one whose motive is duty unmingled with feeling—would be admitted as strictly applicable to the wise man. Any deviation from such a model is censured as a weakness, if not worse. Even compassion, which all moralists would now recognise as essential to the highest type of human excellence, was rejected by the Stoical philosophy as, if not in itself a vice, at least leading by necessary consequence to that which is a vice—" Cadit igitur in eundem et misereri et invidere. Nam qui dolet rebus alicujus adversis, idem alicujus etiam secundis dolet. . . . . In quem igitur cadit misereri, in eundem etiam invidere. Non cadit autem invidere in sapientem: ergo ne misereri quidem."[1] This extirpation of the feeling need not, according to the same philosophy, cause neglect of the *act* which is usually prompted by the feeling. This may be better performed under a sense of duty—" Cur misereare potius quam feras opem, si id facere possis! an sine misericordia liberales esse non possumus? Non enim suscipere ipsi ægritudines propter alios debemus: sed alios, si possumus, levare ægritudine."[2]

It is unnecessary to add that, rejecting emotion as unworthy of man, the Stoics would reject it far more strongly as unworthy of God.

But this idea of the perfection of humanity is a paradox which the general sense of mankind has always refused to accept. Indeed it may well be doubted, whether even those who formed the conception would have approved of it, had they seen it com-

[1] Cicero, *Tusc. Disp.* III., 10.   [2] *Ibid.*, IV., 26.

Is an Emotion a Moral Defect? 157

pletely realized. For we must be careful not to confound *controlled* emotion with *absence* of emotion. The former is very generally an object of admiration not alone to those, if there be now any such, who hold the Stoical theory, but to those who would utterly reject it. And it is quite possible that much of the admiration, which men imagined themselves to have bestowed upon a mind from which emotion was absent, was really given to a mind in which emotion was controlled.

But if this confusion be avoided, the answer which man's moral nature has given to the question—Is an emotion a weakness?—cannot be regarded as uncertain. Take, for example, the emotion which, as we have seen, the Stoical philosophy condemns as almost a vice—compassion. Compare the characters of two men, whose active beneficence is the same, but of whom one *feels* for the distress which he relieves, while the other is insensible to it. The Stoical philosophy prefers the second character, but the general verdict of mankind is quite different. The man who can feel no compassion would be pronounced by the moral sense to be morally deficient, how beneficent soever his actions might be.

Is this verdict limited in its application to *man?* Do we approve of the presence of emotion *in man* and censure its absence, merely because the weakness of human nature renders certain important ends unattainable without emotion? Is emotion, in fact, to be regarded as a supply to certain deficiencies in human nature, and can we not imagine a higher order of beings to whom such a supply would be unnecessary? If this be so, ought we not to regard the absence of emotion in such beings as a mark of moral superiority?

Bishop Butler would, I think, answer this question in the affirmative. He does indeed maintain strongly that, in comparing one *man* with another, emotion ought not to be regarded as a weakness. On the contrary, the removal of this class of mental phenomena would leave a creature like man without a sufficient principle of action. Butler therefore rejects altogether the Stoical theory of the perfection of *human* nature. On the other hand, he does seem to admit the force of the objection which would exclude emotion from any place in a perfect nature. "Are not passion and affection," says Butler, stating the Stoical objection, "themselves a weakness, and what a perfect being must be entirely free from?" To which his reply is—"Perhaps so, but it is mankind I am speaking of, imperfect creatures, and who naturally and from the condition we are placed in, necessarily depend upon each other. With respect to such creatures it would be found of as bad consequence to eradicate all natural affections as to be entirely governed by them. This would almost sink us to the condition of brutes, and that would leave us without a sufficient principle of action. . . . . . Neither is affection itself at all a weakness, nor does it argue defect, any otherwise than as our senses and appetites do; they belong to our condition of nature, and are what we cannot do without." In this passage he certainly admits it to be at least probable that a nature more perfect than that of man may be marked by a complete absence of emotion. With regard to the Divine Nature, Butler's language is still more clear—"God Almighty is, to be sure, unmoved by passion or appetite, unchanged by affection. . . . . It is a real . . . . absurdity to endeavour to eradicate the passions He has given us, because He is without them."[1]

A minute criticism of this passage might show that it is not absolutely inconsistent with a belief in the existence of *affection*, as distinguished from passion or appetite, in the Divine Nature. Still I suppose that Butler *did* mean to exclude it. But if it be true that absence of emotion is essential to a perfect nature,

[1] Sermon V., pp. 86-7 (Carmichael's edition).

Is an Emotion a Moral Defect? 159

why should not the moral faculty approve of a *human* nature in which this mark of perfection is found combined with active benevolence? It is nothing to say that this combination does not exist in man. The moral sense can judge perfectly well of an imaginary character, provided that there be nothing essentially discordant in the elements of which the picture consists. There is no such discordance here; nay, the combination is one which is often approximately realized in those whom use has familiarized with scenes of sorrow, blunting their sensibilities, yet without diminishing their active benevolence. And the question which we have to ask is—Do we consider the moral character to be exalted by the insensibility which is thus produced? Nay rather, do we not regard this insensibility as the *price* which the actively benevolent must pay for the power of practical usefulness which their sad experience has given them? And if we could find a man who had gained the practical power without losing the emotion, should we not regard him as morally superior to one who had, in the process, become callous to human suffering, although not neglectful of it? No one is more familiar with scenes of sorrow than a physician. Witnessing those scenes, perhaps daily, he can hardly avoid the gradual weakening of the "passive impressions" (to use Butler's words) which generally attends such experiences. Yet when we find, as we sometimes do, a physician who has not paid this price for his powers of practical usefulness—whose emotions are still fresh—who can pity as well as relieve, do we not attribute to him a moral character, not exceptionally low but exceptionally high? Do we despise him because he feels for the suffering which he is striving to alleviate? God forbid.

It is plain, then, that the approval which the benevolent affections receive from the moral faculty is not given solely on account of their results. They are approved for their own sake.

These affections form an essential part of the loftiest ideal of *human* character which we are capable of forming. By what process, then, do we arrive at an ideal of a *super*human character which excludes this element? It seems difficult to answer this question.

It may be objected that emotion necessarily implies passivity, and cannot therefore be ascribed to God, who is, as Locke says, above all passive power. To this, however, it may fairly be replied that perception implies passivity quite as much as emotion. "In bare naked perception," says Locke, "the mind is, for the most part, only passive."[1] This is evidently true. For perception is the effect produced on the mind by the presence of an external object (if there be such a thing); and when we speak of "an effect produced on the mind" we speak of the mind as passive. The truth is that we cannot conceive a mind which is destitute of passive power to be conscious of the existence of anything distinct from itself. We are obliged, therefore, in considering the relation of the Divine Being to other beings, and to things, to make one of the following suppositions:—
1. There is nothing distinct from God. This is Pantheism.
2. The Divine Mind is unconscious of the existence or actions of any being but Himself. No one, I presume, would accept this supposition. 3. The Divine Mind is not destitute of passive power. If we attempt to escape from this logical dilemma, by declaring that the whole matter is beyond the grasp of human thought, and that, in some way inconceivable by us, the Divine Mind may perceive without the possession of passive power, we must be aware that the ascription of emotion to the Divine Mind may be similarly defended. If the consideration of our limited powers of thought requires us to admit, that perception in the Divine Mind does not necessarily imply passive

---

[1] *Essay*, Book II., chap. ix., sec. 1.

power, why should not the same consideration require us to admit that, in the Divine Mind, the possession of passive power need not be implied by the presence of emotion? To our minds both suppositions are inconceivable.

I conclude this note with the following deeply significant words of F. W. Newman :—

" To endeavour to resolve God into intellect without affections is Atheism under a new name; for mere intellect is not an active principle."[1]

NOTE H, PAGE 38.

WHAT IS A MIRACLE?[2]

"The fundamental conception, which is indispensable to a true apprehension of the nature of a miracle, is that of the distinction of Mind from Matter, and of the power of the former, as a personal, conscious, and free agent, to influence the pheno-

---

[1] *The Soul*, p. 42.
[2] The definition of a miracle here given has evoked a certain amount of opposing (though very friendly) criticism. This criticism has taken most definite shape in the *Church Quarterly Review* for January of the present year (1879). The reviewer (to whom, as indeed to all my reviewers, I desire to return my best thanks for their very favourable notices of the first edition of the present work) objects :—

1. That I have left no room for the function of the secondary causes which may intervene between the volition and the accomplishment of it. Where, he asks, is the *nexus* of secondary causes to be broken in order to introduce the supposed immediate volition? (The objection is rather anticipated than alleged by the reviewer.)

2. That the asserted facts of electro-biology are inconsistent with the supposition that man's will, without the intervention of man's body, has no power over external nature.

3. That there is no generic distinction between the power of spirit over the particular system of matter forming the human body and its power over

mena of the latter. We are conscious of this power in ourselves; we experience it in our every-day life: but we experience also its restriction within certain narrow limits, the principal one being that man's influence upon foreign bodies is only possible through the instrumentality of his own body. Beyond these limits is the region of the miraculous. In at least the

any other system of matter. (I am not sure that I rightly understand this objection.)

To answer the first question we must inquire—Where and how does *human* volition break the *nexus* of secondary causes? To simplify the inquiry, let it be supposed that there is but one man in the world, and that his will is, for a time, inactive. During this period of inactivity the purely physical causes are producing their full effects. Among these effects some are produced in the body of the man. By the action of the chemical forces there is developed in his body, at every instant, a certain amount of that motion, imperceptible to our senses as motion, which we call heat. Part of this heat passes off, by radiation and otherwise, as heat; while part is transformed into the involuntary motions of the heart, lungs, &c., which we call *vital*. These phenomena are altogether independent of the will, which we have supposed to be inactive. Now, let us suppose that the will becomes active. Let the man will, for example, to move his arm. How does that volition break the *nexus* of purely physical causes? By effecting the transformation of a certain amount of heat into a corresponding amount of sensible motion. The will cannot, as we know, create motion any more than it can create matter. It can but change one kind of motion into another; and the sphere of its direct power of effecting this change does not extend beyond the system of matter which is called the body. It is thus, I conceive, that the *nexus* of purely physical causes is broken by the human will. And this break in the *nexus* does not annul the proper function of the physical causes. These causes are as active as before; and the *nexus* is broken, not by annulling them, but by introducing the transforming energy of the will, as a new element, into the series.

Precisely the same may be said of the interposition of the Divine will, save that it is not, like the human will, limited in its sphere of operation, and that in the Divine interposition there may be, although we cannot certainly say that there always is, a *creation* of motion. The human will can interfere immediately only in one class of phenomena—the Divine will is not bound by this limitation. But the function of the physical causes is not annulled by either interposition.

With regard to the phenomena of electro-biology, I cannot hold it to be proved that there is an immediate action of the will of the operator upon great majority of the miracles recorded in Scripture, the supernatural element appears, not in the relation of matter to matter, but in that of matter to mind; in the exercise of a personal power transcending the limits of man's will. . . .

". . . When a sick man is healed, or a tempest stilled by a word, the mere action of matter upon matter may possibly be

the patient without the intervention of any bodily influence. It does not seem impossible that the will may act primarily upon the body of the person who wills, developing a bodily condition which in turn influences the body of the other. The term "animal magnetism" would seem to indicate that those who adopted it had formed some such idea of the phenomena in question. Now analogy would lead us, in the absence of direct proof, to prefer a theory of these phenomena, which is in accordance with the ordinary operation of the human will, to a theory which assigns to it an operation wholly extraordinary. And if it be true that, in the electro-biological phenomena, there is a direct action of the human will upon a foreign body, it must be admitted that this group of phenomena is quite unique. I do not think that there is evidence sufficient to justify us in attributing to the human will a power so anomalous. The fact may be perfectly real, but the power of the will over foreign matter is not a fact, but a theory devised to account for a fact. I cannot, then, admit that the electro-biological phenomena form a valid exception to that law which appears to govern all other phenomena—that man's will, without the intervention of man's body, is powerless upon external nature.

It has been said that the distinction which I have drawn between Divine and human action does not indicate a difference in kind, inasmuch as there is no such difference between the action of the will upon the particular system of matter forming the human body, and the action of the will upon any other system of matter whatever. I do not know that this can be regarded as an objection. At most, it is only an objection to the use of the word "generic" as applied to the difference (p. 41). We use the word "generic" with a good deal of laxity; and it is, perhaps, impossible to lay down a perfectly definite rule for its correct application. But it must be admitted that there is an enormous gap between the will which can only affect one such system of matter, and the will which can affect all systems of matter in the universe. Whether this gap ought or ought not to be called "generic" is only a question with regard to the proper application of a word. Whatever we are to call it, the "gulf" is enormous, and apparently impassable. I should hesitate to say the same of any other difference which exists between a miracle and an ordinary phenomenon.

similar to that which takes place when the same effects occur in a natural way: the miracle consists in the means by which that action is brought about."[1]

This statement of the essential difference of a miracle agrees with that given in the text, namely, that the difference consists in the immediate sequence of an external result to a volition.

Professor Mansel elsewhere uses expressions which seem to imply that a miracle *may be* a violation of the laws of nature.

"A miracle, in one sense, need not be necessarily a violation of the laws of nature. God may make use of natural instruments, acting after their kind."[2]

I have endeavoured to show (pp. 41-2) that the adoption of natural instruments makes no change in the essential character of the action.

Professor Baden Powell seems to adopt the same conception. Speaking of natural phenomena, which still remain inexplicable, he says:—

"None of these or the like instances are at all of the same kind, or have any characteristic in common with the idea of what is implied by the term 'miracle,' which is asserted to mean something at variance with nature and law."[3]

Bishop Butler's opinion might appear at first sight to be nearly the same—

"A miracle, in its very notion, is relative to a course of nature; and implies somewhat different from it; considered as being so."[4]

But it must be observed that, although miracles are here stated to be *different* from a course of nature, they are not said to be *contrary* to it; and Butler's account of the matter is quite consistent with the supposition, that a miracle implies no more

---

[1] *Aids to Faith*, pp. 20-21. [2] *Limits of Religious Thought*, pp. 128-9.
[3] *Essays and Reviews*, p. 109. [4] *Analogy*, p. 80 (Fitzgerald's edition).

What is a Miracle?

than the exertion of a force not included among the ordinary forces of nature; and that it is, therefore, in a certain sense, different from a course of nature, as including an element not contained therein.

This distinction is marked by Archbishop Trench—
"But while the miracle is not thus nature, so neither is it *against* nature. That language, however commonly in use, is yet wholly unsatisfactory, which speaks of these wonderful works of God as *violations* of a natural law. *Beyond* nature, *beyond* and *above* the nature which we know, they are, but not contrary to it." [1]

The following statement of the same author seems to be less accurate:—

"We should term the miracle not the infraction of a law, but behold in it the lower law neutralized, and for the time put out of working by an higher; and of this, abundant analogous examples are evermore going forward before our eyes. Continually we behold in the world around us lower laws held in restraint by higher, mechanic by dynamic, chemical by vital, physical by moral; yet we say not, when the lower thus gives place in favour of the higher, that there was any violation of law, or that anything contrary to nature came to pass;—rather, we acknowledge the law of a greater freedom swallowing up the law of a lesser. Thus, when I lift my arm, the law of gravitation is not, as far as my arm is concerned, denied or annihilated; it exists as much as ever, but is held in suspense by the higher law of my will. The chemical laws which would bring about decay in animal substances still subsist, even when they are hemmed in and hindered by the salt which keeps those substances from corruption." [2]

The word "law" appears to me to be in this passage incor-

[1] *Notes on the Miracles*, p. 15.   [2] *Ibid.*, pp. 15, 16.

rectly used. Two *forces* may oppose each other, and we may even speak of them as "higher" and "lower." But two *laws* cannot be opposed. If they appear to be so, either the opposition is unreal, or one of the asserted laws is untrue. Thus, in the example which the Archbishop gives, the *force* of the muscle is opposed to the *force* of gravity. But there is no opposition between the *laws* of these forces. The law of gravitation does not assert that a heavy body will necessarily fall, but only that there is a force urging it downwards, which will produce its proper effect, unless it be resisted by an opposing force of sufficient magnitude. Much of the discredit which has been thrown upon the reality of miracles may be traced to the neglect of this distinction. Miracles have been declared to be incredible because they were supposed to involve a violation of the laws of nature. The truth is, not that a *law* of nature has been violated or suspended, but that a *force* of nature has been overcome by the action of a stronger force. We may neglect this distinction in Theology, but we are careful to observe it in our every-day life. To resist the *laws* of nature is the act of a lunatic. To resist the *forces* of nature is the very condition of man's existence. It is true that this is in general done by opposing one force of nature to another. But the intervention of man's will is an essential part of the process, and without this intervention the forces of nature would speedily terminate his existence. The cold of one winter's night would be enough to kill the strongest man alive, were not this force of nature resisted by the exertion of his will. It is true that we can oppose this natural force (using the word "cold" in a popular sense) only by making use of forces quite as natural, namely, the non-conducting property of certain bodies, and the heat of fire. But to render the opposition effectual the action of the human will is necessary. In the ordinary works of man, the intervention of his body is required; in a miracle the intervention is unnecessary. In both, a *force* of nature is overcome; in neither, is a *law* of nature violated.

The importance of the common dogma that "God works by means" is strongly insisted on by the Duke of Argyll. Much (if not all) of the difficulty which attends belief in supernatural agency is due, he thinks, to neglect or denial of this truth. Speaking of "that idea of the supernatural which so many reject as inconceivable," he says—"What then is that idea? Have we not traced it to its den at last? By 'supernatural' power, do we not mean power independent of the use of means, as distinguished from power depending on knowledge—even infinite knowledge—of the means proper to be employed?"

"This is the sense—probably the only sense—in which the supernatural is, to many minds, so difficult of belief. No man can have any difficulty in believing that there are natural laws of which he is ignorant; nor in conceiving that there may be Beings who do know them, and can use them, even as he himself now uses the few laws with which he is acquainted. The real difficulty lies in the idea of Will exercised without the use of means—not in the exercise of means which are beyond our knowledge."[1]

Is this true? Is it true that the difficulty, whatever it may be, of accepting an alleged miracle as real would be materially alleviated, if it were shown that natural means had been used for its accomplishment? Thus, for example, in the history of the Egyptian plagues, the locusts are said to have been brought and removed by "natural means," namely, easterly and westerly winds respectively. If any incredibility attach to these asserted events, does the introduction of *machinery* in the plague of locusts render the story of that plague more credible than the story of other plagues, in which no such "natural

[1] *Reign of Law*, p. 14.

means" are said to have been used? Had the coming and departure of the locusts been reported to have followed directly upon the command of God, without the intervention of any wind, would the story have been in any respect more improbable? I cannot think so.

For it will be observed that the introduction of this machinery does not *remove* the direct intervention of God; it merely shifts it back to an earlier part of the series. The east wind brought the locusts; but what brought the east wind? It is as real a miracle that the east wind should come at the direct command of God as it is that the locusts should come without the wind. Whatever difficulties, theological or philosophical, attend the reception of the one story, attend also the reception of the other. So it is, too, in every similar case. The immediate consequent of the special exertion of the Divine volition is a *miracle*. Between the immediate consequent and the final result any number of terms—"means," as we call them—may be interposed, and the multiplication of these terms serves to hide from our eyes the real nature of the event. Men may think that they are softening away its miraculous character by insisting on the consideration that "God works by means." But this is not true. The miraculous character is not *altered* by this consideration; it is only disguised. A miracle is not the less a miracle because, in the series of phenomena which we call an event, there are present, in addition to the one miraculous element, a hundred elements which are not miraculous.

Note I, Page 41.

ILLOGICAL DISTINCTION BETWEEN THE WORLD OF SPIRIT AND THE WORLD OF MATTER.

The impossibility of rejecting, as inconsistent with the universality of Law, the interference of God in the world of matter, while admitting the possibility of such interference in the world of spirit, is very forcibly stated by the Duke of Argyll—

"Will this reasoning bear analysis? Can the distinction it assumes be maintained? Whatever difficulties there may be in reconciling the ideas of Law and of Volition are difficulties which apply equally to the worlds of matter and of mind. The mind is as much subject to Law as the body is. The Reign of Law is over all, and if its dominion be really incompatible with the agency of Volition, Human or Divine, then the mind is as inaccessible to that agency as material things."[1]

It is hard to see how the principle here laid down can be disputed. When we ask God to grant us a spiritual benefit, we ask Him to intervene in the sequence of mental phenomena. If a change in the sequence of phenomena produced by the intervention of the Divine Will be a violation of Law, we are asking for a violation of Law; and this violation is equally real or equally unreal whether the interrupted sequence be in the world of matter or in the world of mind.

Note K, Page 46.

INHERENT SUPERIORITY OF MIND OVER MATTER.

The position taken in the text with regard to the inherent superiority of mind over matter is altogether independent of

[1] *Reign of Law*, p. 61.

the question, whether mind may not be itself a modification of matter. It is enough for my present purpose, that mankind have adopted the division of the forces by which the phenomena of the world are produced into two great classes, to which they have given the names, mental and material; and that the difference between these classes is sufficiently marked to justify the classification as at least convenient. This principle is quite familiar to us in the world of Science. We agree to place in separate classes the force of heat and the force of electricity. But we do not thereby decide the question whether these forces may not be different modifications of a single force. Even if this be true, the phenomena resulting from these modifications respectively are so different as to justify a separate classification of their causes.

So, too, in the present case. We may speak of the superiority of mind over matter, without deciding the question whether mind and matter be modifications of the same substance. If this be true, the meaning of the assertion will be, that the forces of that modification which we call mind show a constant and ever-increasing tendency to prevail over the forces of that other modification which we call matter.

It may be contended, in opposition to this statement, that mind prevails over matter only by arraying the forces of matter against each other; and that mind without the aid of matter is powerless, whereas matter without the aid of mind has still very great power. But it must be remembered that our present question is not whether the powers of the mind require for their development the aid of matter, but whether it be not true that the mind possesses powers which (so far as we can judge) cannot be *transferred* to any system of matter. It is true that mind prevails against matter by the power which it possesses of arraying the forces of matter against each other. We do not overcome the force of fire by a thought, but by opposing to it another material force—the force of water. But the power of arraying the material forces against each other—the power of forming new combinations among the forces which exist around us, and thus compelling them to produce the result which the combiner wishes—the power of *invention*, as we usually call it—appears to be exclusively the prerogative of mind. Man, who himself possesses a large measure of this power, has never been able to transfer it in the smallest degree to a material combination. We may not, perhaps, pronounce such a transference to be impossible, for we are rarely justified in pronouncing any thing to be impossible. But we are justified in saying that the history of mechanism, wonderful as it is, gives no indication of the possibility of such a transference. The exquisite machine of the nineteenth century is as far from possessing the power of invention as was the knife of the stone period.

Closely akin to the power of invention, and, apparently, as little capable of being transferred from mind to matter, is the power of *cumulative* improvement. Only the mental powers seem to be capable of deriving benefit from *experience*. Only the mental powers are strengthened and enlarged by knowledge—by knowledge of that which other mental powers have done, or tried to do. It would be an exaggeration of the truth to say that this privilege is absolutely limited to man. Many of the lower animals do to some small extent profit by experience. But cumulative improvement—the power of transmitting the experience of one generation to the next, so that the benefit derived from such experience may constantly increase—this seems to be peculiar to the mind of man.

On the whole, we are justified in saying that mind possesses powers which appear to be intransferable to matter—that these peculiar powers enable—and, so far as we can judge from all the evidence which we possess, will always enable—mind to triumph over matter, not indeed directly, but by arraying the forces of matter against each other. It is the possession of these peculiar powers which justifies the claim of superiority so commonly made on behalf of mental as against material forces; and the power, which mind possesses, of transmitting the result of its experience, and thus of securing a constant increase of mental force, makes it in a high degree probable that this superiority will become every day more marked.

The case imagined in the text, namely, the transference of the powers possessed by the man of the nineteenth century to the machine of the thirtieth, is conceivable only when understood with a certain limitation. There are, as we have seen, powers which we cannot conceive to be so transferred. We cannot conceive an inventing machine, nor a machine which will improve itself by observation and experience. We cannot conceive a machine which will adapt itself (unless by accident) to a combination of circumstances unforeseen by the contriver. We cannot therefore conceive it to be possible that man of any age, how great soever its intellectual development may be, should construct a machine capable of fully replacing the *man* of any other age, however rude.

But it may be argued that this very impossibility of transferring his powers to a machine is itself the result of man's imperfection. It is true—it may be said—that we cannot conceive a machine capable of fulfilling (except by accident) a purpose which was not contemplated by its designer. Man can adapt himself to a new state of circumstances; but the machine which man has made cannot. But the very expression "a new state of circumstances" marks a human imperfection. If man possessed the power of foreseeing the future, there could be for him no such thing as a new state of circumstances. Gifted with this power, might he not, conceivably at least, construct a machine which could do all that he himself could do? And if this be a conceivable power in man, does it not necessarily exist in God?

In answering this question we must observe that the field of man's activity is twofold. Human actions affect either the systems of matter by which he is surrounded, or the minds of other beings like himself. It is only in the former of these fields that he can, even conceivably, be replaced by a machine. We *may* conceive the physical effects which are now produced by the action of man to be produced by a skilfully contrived machine, but we cannot conceive a similar substitution to be successful in the moral world. There, the effect depends not only on the thing done, but on the *manner* in which, and the agent by which, it is done. The machine and the sentient being may produce the same physical phenomenon, but the moral effect of the two actions will be wholly different. Even when both actions proceed from sentient beings, the moral effect of an action which partakes in any considerable degree of a mechanical character will differ widely from that of an action which does not contain this element. Compare, for example, the moral effect of relief given by individual kindness with that of relief given under a poor-law. Nor would this difference be obliterated, even if the poor-law arrangements were known by the recipients of relief to be the work of a benevolent despot, actuated solely by desire for the welfare of his people. No general system, be it never so perfect, can replace individual kindness in its moral effects. But as I have spoken of this subject more fully elsewhere, I need only remark, that this difference between a sentient being and a machine appears to us to be indelible. That such a being should be able to transfer to a system of mechanism the moral influence over the minds of men, which he himself possesses, is to us absolutely inconceivable.

174   *Appendix—The Statistical Argument.*

NOTE L, PAGE 68.

THE STATISTICAL ARGUMENT.

Very different opinions have been expressed by those who have treated of the efficacy of prayer, as to the applicability of this species of argument to such a question. Before examining the particular specimen adduced in the present case, some have declared the statistical argument to be wholly inapplicable, while others have maintained that it is absolutely decisive. Dr. Hessey and Mr. Galton may be taken to represent the opposite poles of opinion. "To resort," says the former, "to statistics in such a matter is an absolute mistake, and we must recommend those whose tastes lead them to such inquiries, to apply them to other matters on which they may be legitimately and profitably employed."[1] On the other hand, Mr. Galton thinks that the question ought to be decided altogether by statistics.

"The collapse of the argument of universality leaves us solely concerned with a simple statistical question—are prayers answered or are they not?"[2] With regard to the first position, I have already said that I believe it to be untenable. The objections against the use of the statistical argument, which Dr. Hessey and others have founded on the undoubted fact that there are connected with each case certain important details, of which we are necessarily ignorant, prove no more than this, that, as we are obliged to assume things which we cannot strictly prove, the argument ought not to be considered decisive. But the rejection of the argument as inapplicable, *because* it is founded on statistics, cannot be justified. A theory which professes to find a connexion between two classes of phenomena, both of which are to some extent within the cognizance of the human

[1] *Boyle Lectures* for 1873, p. 116.
[2] *Fortnightly Review*, vol. xii. (new series), p. 126.

intellect, may be tested with more or less accuracy by observation and comparison of these phenomena—in other words, by statistics.

On the other hand, the proposal to set aside all other arguments and decide the question by statistics alone is quite as unreasonable. This monopoly can be justified only in two cases—namely, when the selected argument has the force of demonstration, or when the rejected arguments are wholly devoid of weight. Mr. Galton does not actually *say* this of arguments drawn from the teaching of Scripture or the teaching of Christ: he does not indeed mention these arguments at all. But when, after having, as he conceives, disposed of the argument from the general consent of mankind, he declares the question to be *solely* one of statistics, it is plain that he regards the other arguments as of no value whatever. I need hardly say that no Christian controversialist could consent to conduct the discussion on these principles. If the teaching and example of Christ on such a point as this are to be set aside, not even because they are outweighed by other considerations, but because they are in themselves valueless, the Christian religion cannot be said to exist. Mr. Leslie Stephen's question—Are we Christians?—must be answered in the negative; and it is hardly worth while to defend *one* doctrine in the general collapse of Christianity. I must premise, therefore, in examining Mr. Galton's arguments, that I cannot admit the reasonableness of the monopoly which he claims for the statistical argument. I pass by, at this stage of the discussion, the reasoning by which Mr. Galton seeks to justify his rejection of the argument from general consent. The examination of this reasoning will find a more fitting place when I come to consider the argument itself: for the present I would only observe that, in noticing *any* other argument, Mr. Galton seems to admit that the statistical argument is not absolutely decisive. I do not think that all those who agree with

176   *Appendix—The Statistical Argument.*

Mr. Galton's conclusion would admit so much. "We do not want to know," say a great many, "what has been taught as truth, or what we may expect to be true. We want to know what *is* true. Statistics can tell us that, and we will not listen to any other argument."

If this claim to a monopoly in the decision of every question to which they are applicable be a just claim, it must be confessed that statistics are greatly belied by the common proverb that "you can prove anything by figures." But the truth is, that the assurance derivable from statistics varies with the circumstances of the case, from the faintest presumption up to a probability so strong as to be indistinguishable from certainty. There are, undoubtedly, cases in which all would concede a monopoly to the statistical argument by refusing a hearing to any other. No one would listen to an *à priori* argument against the conclusion that drunkenness is the cause of disease, crime, and misery. If such an argument were advanced, men would say, "It can be shown by statistics that the fact is real, and we do not care to hear an argument which could at most only show that this fact is *à priori* improbable." This answer is quite reasonable in a case where the statistical argument is so strong as to leave no doubt on the mind of any one, but would be altogether *un*reasonable in a great number of cases to which statistics can be applied, but with results far less decisive. In such cases the rejection of *à priori* arguments cannot be justified.

The concession of an absolute superiority over *à priori* arguments, which so many are willing to make to the argument from statistics, is probably due to the fact that this argument professes to tell us what *has* happened; whereas *à priori* arguments only profess to tell what may be *expected* to happen or to have happened. The very form of expression of the second class of arguments shows that only a *probable* conclusion can be derived from them; whereas in the other the form of expression appears to promise certainty, and not unfrequently obtains the credit of that which it seems to promise. The truth is, however, as the Calculus of Probabilities proves, that statistics *never* give absolute certainty. Indeed the very nature of the argument, which is essentially cumulative, shows that it can only lead to a probable conclusion. The probability may be so high as to give an assurance which is practically equivalent to certainty; but it is a probability still, and may be a very slight probability. To reject all other arguments in favour of that derived from statistics, before we have even ascertained what amount of probability this argument can give, is therefore inconsistent with the principles of just reasoning.

In examining the several statistical arguments adduced by Mr. Galton, I must take exception to the principles which he lays down for the guidance of the inquiry.

"The principles are broad and simple upon which our inquiry into the efficacy of prayer must be established. We must gather cases for statistical comparison, in which the same object is keenly pursued by two classes similar in their physical, but opposite in their spiritual state; the one class being prayerful, the other materialistic. Prudent pious people must be compared with prudent materialistic people, and not with the imprudent nor the vicious."[1]

The adoption of this principle would exclude from consideration all cases in which the accomplishment of the petitioner's desire is effected by means which we usually call "natural." Thus, for example, if the thing asked for be worldly prosperity, the prayer may be answered by giving to the petitioner a larger measure of the mental qualities by which worldly prosperity is secured—by rendering him more intelligent or more cautious. Mr. Galton, by refusing to compare *prudent* persons who pray with *imprudent* persons who do not pray, in effect discards all

[1] *Fortnightly Review*, ut supra, p. 126.

such cases from consideration. Such a principle would admit no prayer to be successful which was not the *immediate* antecedent to the acquisition by the supplicant of that for which he prays. If the immediate antecedent be a phenomenon which, in the ordinary sequence of events, usually precedes that which is the subject of the prayer, Mr. Galton's principle would require us to exclude such a case from our statistical inquiry.

Statistics thus obtained are inapplicable to the Christian theory—perhaps to any theory—of prayer. It is not asserted that in every case of successful prayer the blessing follows immediately on the petition, without the intervention of any other phenomenon. On the contrary, the common saying, that "God works by means," indicates the usual expectation of certain intervening steps between the Divine volition and the accomplishment of the petitioner's desire. All prayers which are thus answered would be, according to Mr. Galton's principle, classed as unsuccessful—a classification which is obviously unjust. I cannot think, therefore, that any valid argument against the efficacy of prayer can be founded on statistics so obtained. It is right to observe, however, that the special statistics which Mr. Galton has adduced are not open to this objection. But the remark does apply with a certain amount of force to some of his more general arguments. Thus prayer for the recovery of a sick person may be answered either by giving a more than ordinary effect to the treatment which has been adopted, or by suggesting a better treatment to the mind of the physician. Suppose the prayer to be answered in the second way. The physician has no means of distinguishing such a suggestion from the ordinary prompting of his own mind. The amendment of the sick person would be the immediate consequent, not of the prayer, but of the application of a new remedy. Statistics collected as Mr. Galton proposes to collect them would take no cognizance of the intervention of prayer in such a series. Mr.

Galton would refuse to compare the number of cases of recovery under one kind of treatment with the number of cases of recovery under a different kind of treatment. The difference of treatment might be itself the result of prayer, but it would not be attributed to prayer. The recovery of the sick person would be ascribed simply to its immediate antecedents—namely, the particular medical treatment employed; and this treatment itself would be, if any cause were sought, ascribed to the genius or learning of the physician, unaided by any supernatural power. In such a case prayer might have a real effect, and yet no trace of the effect would appear in a statistical return.

But the attempt to deduce a conclusion with regard to the efficacy of prayer from the statistics of recovery is attended by another difficulty. It has been said—How are we to distinguish real from unreal prayer? We see hundreds—thousands—assume the attitude and the words of supplication. What statistical return can tell us how many of them really pray? But, in such a case as that which we are now considering, shall we not rather ask, How many do *not* pray? How many are there, at least among Theists, whose scepticism is proof against the sight of one they love hanging between life and death? Man may be sceptical in calmer moments, but is he sceptical then? The impulse which turns his eyes to heaven—the cry for help which rises to his lips—are these things confined to the "religious world"? The controversialist may condemn these impulses as irrational, comparing them to the mournful cry of a dumb animal when in pain. But the question here is not, Are these things irrational? but, Are they real? If they *are* real, where shall we look for any account, approaching to accuracy, of the unprayed-for sick? If we assume that none are prayed for except those whose friends are habitually religious, I believe that we shall be very wide of the truth.

There are, then, as it seems to me, two elements of uncertainty in arguments against the efficacy of prayer derived from the statistics of recovery from sickness. In the first place, such statistics would take no account of cases, if such existed, in which the effect of prayer was shown, not directly, but by the intervention of a natural agent; and in the second place, they would reckon as unprayed-for recoveries, and therefore as instances adverse to the efficacy of prayer, many cases in which real prayer had been made.

But I need not dwell further on this argument, as I do not suppose that there are any accurate statistics of the percentages of recovery among persons whose friends are religious, as compared with similar percentages among those whose friends are not religious. Mr. Galton's argument is here only indirectly statistical. "Physicians," he says, "do not believe in the efficacy of prayer. A class of men who are most deeply interested in watching for every influence, favourable or injurious, which can affect the progress of disease, have systematically ignored the influence of prayer. If this influence were real, must they not know it? If they believed it to be real, would they not urge the use of this, as they would of any other means which might promote the recovery of their patients? If they do not so urge it, is it not because they do not believe?"

Does not this argument prove too much? Are there *no* physicians who believe in the efficacy of prayer? It is certainly a very common article of faith in the Christian world? Is it rejected by the whole medical world? If there be physicians who believe in the efficacy of prayer, why do *they* not urge its importance upon the friends of their patients? Because, replies in effect Mr. Galton, they do not really believe it. "Although they have heard it insisted on from childhood upwards, they are unable to detect its influence."[1] Mr. Galton does not, of course,

---

[1] Page 127.

The Statistical Argument. 181

mean that a physician will use no remedy unless he has personally "detected its influence." Enough for him that from whatever reason—personal experience, the experience of other men, or a knowledge of the general properties of the proposed remedy—he *believes* that this remedy will have a beneficial effect. Mr. Galton's explanation of the fact that physicians do not usually insist upon the importance of prayer cannot mean less than this—that their belief is unreal.

Now Mr. Galton can hardly doubt that very many of those to whom he attributes unbelief would flatly contradict him. He may say that they do not know themselves, and that they are dignifying with the name of belief that which is no more than a traditional idea, whose correctness it has never occurred to them to question. But, as no man can look into the mind of another, the fact remains, that Mr. Galton's mode of explaining the silence of physicians as to the importance of prayer obliges him to make an assertion with regard to the belief of other men, which the men themselves—the only possible witnesses upon the subject—would deny without hesitation.

But it may be said, This is an inference, not an assertion; and if you dispute its truth, you are bound to point out the fallacy in the process by which it is inferred. To this it may be replied, in the first place, that whether it be an assertion or an inference, its truth is open to grave suspicion if it be opposed to the testimony of those whose state of mind it professes to describe. If it be a logical inference, this doubt necessarily attaches to one or both of the premises from which it is inferred. Now Mr. Galton's argument may be logically stated as follows:—

Physicians habitually urge upon the friends of their patients the practice of everything which they regard as important to the patient's recovery.

But they do not habitually urge the practice of prayer.

Therefore they do not regard prayer as important to the recovery of their patients.

Of these premises the minor is, I suppose, generally, though not universally, true. But certainly the same cannot be said of the major premiss. Physicians do not habitually urge the practice of *every* thing which they regard as important to the recovery of their patients. There is nothing, for example, more important than kindness and love on the part of the friends who surround the sick man's bed. Yet I do not suppose that physicians habitually urge upon them the medical importance of kindness: and the reason of this silence is not, certainly, that they regard kindness as *un*important, but that they assume as a matter of course, unless they have proof of the contrary, that the friends of the sufferer *will* be kind to him.

So, too, in the case of prayer. That a person who has faith, even a weak faith, in its efficacy, will pray for one he loves when attacked by a dangerous illness, is as certain as that one of an affectionate disposition will be kind to him. The physician who himself believes in the efficacy of prayer knows this perfectly. He knows that it is quite as superfluous to exhort a person, who has even a small measure of this faith, to pray for a suffering friend as it would be to exhort one of a loving disposition to be kind to him. Even a clergyman would probably consider any very strenuous exhortation to the practice of this duty unnecessary. He knows that at such a moment submission, not prayer, is the really difficult task.

But if the friend be an absolute *dis*believer in the efficacy of prayer, the exhortation would be useless, for another reason. Such a person could not pray, except as an experiment; and if the physician holds the Christian theory on the subject, he knows that experimental prayer will not succeed.

On the whole, I do not think that it can be reasonably inferred from the silence of physicians, as to the efficacy of prayer,

The Statistical Argument. 183

that they really disbelieve it. And I am sure that there are very many who would, for themselves, reject such an assertion as wholly untrue.

Passing now to Mr. Galton's statistics proper, I observe, in the first place, that before we can apply the Method of Differences to establish the action, or inaction, of a particular cause, we must be satisfied that between the classes compared there is but one *class* difference which is capable of producing the difference of effect observed. Where these precautions have been neglected, the most absurd and contradictory results have been deduced from facts which were in themselves true. Quite recently, for example, writers and speakers have been marshalling facts for the purpose of proving that vaccination augments both the extent and the virulence of the small-pox epidemic. Results like these, obtained generally by a disregard of the necessary precaution mentioned above, have often brought upon the statistical method a large amount of discredit, finding its common expression in the well-known proverb which I have before quoted. But this discredit is unjust. It attaches to the abuse, not the use, of the statistical argument. The method of statistics is no more responsible for the absurdities which men professing to use it, while neglectful of its true principles, have seemed to deduce, than is the science of logic for the fallacies which their authors have affected to clothe in logical forms.

I cannot think that Mr. Galton has been careful to observe the rule which I have stated. Thus, for example, in order to show that prayers for longevity have no effect, he quotes certain statistical returns which appear to prove that members of royal families are in reality more short-lived than ordinary men, although they have in a more than ordinary degree the benefit of the prayers of the community. Now this argument is open to the objection stated above. It makes an assumption with regard to the effect of *class* differences which is purely hypothetical. Mr. Galton, indeed, makes the same assertion of those who maintain the efficacy of prayer. Hypothesis is, he thinks, necessary to make *their* position tenable. Thus, after proving, as he supposes, that members of royal families are more than ordinarily short-lived, he says: "The prayer has, therefore, no efficacy, unless the very questionable hypothesis be raised, that the conditions of royal life may naturally be yet more fatal, and that their influence is partly, though incompletely, neutralized by the effect of public prayers."[1]

On this statement I have to observe that, in laying hypothesis to the charge of his opponents, Mr. Galton mistakes his logical position. The statistical argument is *his*, not theirs. It is he who, if he would make it an *argument*, and not a mere collection of facts, is constrained to assume a principle, namely this, that if prayer be set aside, the other class differences would produce exactly the effect which the facts show to *be* produced. This is a pure hypothesis, and, so far as I can see, without foundation, unless the inefficacy of prayer be already admitted. We have no right to select one of a number of asserted causes and declare it to be inefficacious, because the total effect of all the causes is contrary to that which this single cause, acting by itself, would have produced. Thus, for example, suppose it to be admitted (it is probably true) that royal children receive more than average care during their childhood. Suppose that a statistician were to argue from this fact, combined with the ascertained length of life in the case of royal families, that care of children was useless or pernicious, every one would feel that his reasoning was illogical. It would at once be replied—No; you have not proved that this care is either useless or pernicious; for it is quite possible that its effect may be more than neutralized by other influences peculiar to the class, and unfavourable to longevity. In the present case, no one, I presume, contends that the lives

[1] Page 128.

of members of royal families are *shortened* by prayer. If, therefore, the *fact* of a shorter duration of life in this class of persons have been ascertained, it is plain that class influences unfavourable to longevity do exist. The sole question is of the *amount* of effect which these influences produce; and it is a pure hypothesis which assigns to them just such an intensity as to produce the exact amount observed, without the intervention of the cause which it is sought to discredit. The average life of members of royal families is shorter, says Mr. Galton, by 6·18 years, than the average life of ordinary gentry. Therefore the prayers for a long life offered up in their behalf have no effect. The "suppressed premiss" (to speak logically) of this argument is, that the other class differences between the members of royal families and ordinary gentry would produce in the average lengths of their lives a difference of 6·18 years—neither more nor less— and this is a pure hypothesis.

It may be objected to the estimate of the longevity of the members of royal families which Mr. Galton has here quoted from Dr. Guy, that it is founded on a too narrow induction; and certainly the number of instances, 97, is somewhat small. Still it is true that if these instances presented only individual differences, the probability, mathematically estimated, would be very considerable that Dr. Guy's figures denote a real class difference. But it must be remembered that the number of families from which these individuals are selected is very much less than the number of the individuals, and that although the number of individuals may be sufficient to obliterate the effect of individual peculiarities, the number of families may be quite *in*sufficient to obliterate the effect of family peculiarities. Two or three short-lived individuals would produce no perceptible effect, but two or three short-lived families might diminish the average quite perceptibly.

Mr. Galton has himself given the instance, to which I have

referred in the text, of the mode in which statistics apparently unfavourable may be met. He refuses, and I think rightly, to accept the superior longevity of the clergy as a proof of the efficacy of prayer for a long life. In this case he recognises fully the truth of the principle, that we have no right to pick out one among a number of co-existing causes, and to ascribe a given effect to that one. Mr. Galton does, indeed, point out certain class differences which tend to lengthen the lives of the clergy. But it is quite as easy, as I have shown in the text, to point out certain class differences which are *un*favourable to their longevity. In fine, then, a statistical argument in favour of the efficacy of prayer drawn from the longer lives of the clergy is invalid. A statistical argument against the efficacy of prayer, drawn from the shorter lives of the members of royal families, is in nowise more valid. In order to construct either argument, it is necessary to make an assumption, with regard to the aggregate effect of the other causes which influence the duration of human life, of which no sufficient proof can be given.

It is necessary to observe here that Mr. Galton quotes certain statistics which might seem to weaken or even reverse any argument drawn from the greater longevity of the clergy. These statistics are derived from the ages at death of clergymen whose lives are recorded in the *Biographical Dictionary;* and they prove, if they prove anything, that whereas ordinary clergymen live longer lives than other ordinary men belonging to the higher classes of society, *eminent* clergymen live shorter lives than other eminent men. But the statistics do not really prove this; and Dr. Guy himself, from whom Mr. Galton quotes, has given the cause of the discrepancy:—"As the Biography is very comprehensive, the ages at death are those of clergymen who have lived at very different periods of time, from the date of the earliest trustworthy records down to the early part of the present century."[1] This consideration would not invalidate Mr.

[1] *Journal of the Statistical Society*, vol. xiv., p. 290.

Galton's inference, if the lives of the other eminent men were taken in the same proportion from the different periods. But this is not even approximately true. In the early centuries a much larger proportion of eminent men were divines than in the later centuries; and therefore the comparison is really made between persons living at different periods marked by different average lengths of human life. No trustworthy inference can be drawn from such a comparison.

On the whole, a detailed examination of Mr. Galton's reasoning appears to me to justify the conclusions already stated.

The statistical argument is theoretically applicable to every case in which the relation of cause and effect, or of condition and result, is supposed to exist between two phenomena which are, more or less completely, within the range of human knowledge. In all such cases the application of the "Method of Differences" is perfectly logical, if the logical conditions of that method have been fulfilled. If we can find two classes sufficiently numerous to obliterate the effect of *individual* differences, and whose only *class* difference consists in the presence of the alleged cause in one class and its absence from the other, the statistics of such classes ought to tell us whether the cause does really produce the effect ascribed to it. I conceive, therefore, that Mr. Galton has a perfect *theoretical* right to apply the statistical argument to such a question as that of the efficacy of prayer. But, in the practical application of this argument, I cannot think that he has successfully realized the conditions imposed by the Method of Differences. The classes of lives which he compares have, quite independently of prayer, class differences which affect length of life. His own statistics prove it—nay, he is himself obliged to rely upon the existence of those differences, lest an inference favourable to the efficacy of prayer might be drawn from some of the statistics which he has adduced. And in the case to which he seems to attach most weight, it is plain that, if any general conclusion can be drawn from the statistics, a class difference unfavourable to longevity does exist, and the whole question relates to the *amount* of the effect which it produces. That this amount is precisely the same as it would be if prayers were discontinued may be true; but it is not an inference—it is a hypothesis.

Without, then, denying all weight to Mr. Galton's statistical argument against the efficacy of prayer, the assertion that it is conclusive of the question, or even very strong, appears to me to be untenable.

NOTE M, PAGE 79.

ARGUMENT FROM THE GENERAL CONSENT OF MANKIND.

I have endeavoured to show (App., pp. 122, *et seq.*) that, to each individual, his own undoubting belief is his ultimate criterion of truth, inasmuch as it is the mental effect by which only he can recognise the presence of the cause, objective truth. The question which I have now to consider is a different one. That we must give weight to our own belief is a truism, amounting to no more than this—that we must believe that which we believe. What weight we ought to attach to the belief of another, merely because it is his belief, or whether we should attach to it any weight at all, are wholly different questions.

Different, however, as these questions are from that which has been already considered, they have an intimate and necessary connexion with it. If each man is obliged to adopt, as his criterion of objective truth, his own undoubting belief, he cannot reject as devoid of weight the undoubting belief of other men, without exalting his own intellect into an exceptional position to which it is in nowise entitled. A sentence which condemns as valueless the judgment of mankind generally, making at the same time an exception in favour of one individual, cannot be reasonably defended. A sentence which makes no exception implies universal scepticism.

I have said in the text (p. 85) that the general agreement of mankind is a phenomenon which requires to be accounted for; and that the truth of the proposition in which they agree is *a* mode of accounting for the agreement. In the absence, therefore, of any other plausible explanation of the phenomenon, we are bound to attach considerable weight to the general agreement of mankind, as evidence of the truth of the proposition. So much is, in principle, admitted by Mr. Mill, although the actual amount of weight which he would concede to this argument appears to be small. Thus, in discussing the change in the intellectual attitude of thoughtful unbelievers towards the religious ideas of mankind, he says :—

"This tendency of recent speculation to look upon human opinions pre-eminently from an historical point of view, as facts obeying laws of their own, and requiring, like other observed facts, an historical or a scientific explanation (a tendency not confined to religious subjects), is by no means to be blamed, but to be applauded; not solely as drawing attention to an important and previously neglected aspect of human opinions, but because it has a real though indirect bearing upon the question of their truth. For, whatever opinion a person may adopt on any subject that admits of controversy, his assurance, if he be a cautious thinker, cannot be complete unless he is able to account for the existence of the opposite opinion. To ascribe it to the weakness of the human understanding is an explanation which cannot be sufficient for such a thinker, *for he will be slow to assume that he has himself a less share of that infirmity than the rest of mankind, and that error is more likely to be on the other side than on his own.* In his examination of evidence, the persuasion of others, perhaps of mankind in general, is one of the data of the case—one of the phenomena to be accounted for. As the human intellect, though weak, is not essentially perverted, there is a certain presumption of the truth of any opinion held by many human minds, requiring to be rebutted by assigning some other real or possible cause for its prevalence."—*Essay on Theism*, pp. 127, 128.

I may here remark, with special reference to the sentence which I have italicized, that such an assumption as Mr. Mill here speaks of, even were it allowable, would be wholly insufficient to justify rejection of the belief of other men as devoid of weight. We have seen that each man's undoubting belief is, for him, the ultimate criterion of truth. It is a mental phenomenon which includes a reference to objective truth as its cause. This connexion between the internal and the external phenomenon is one which, by a necessity of our nature, we are compelled to recognise. Were this recognition to cease, the result would be absolute scepticism. Now, denial of all weight to the belief of other men is equivalent to refusal to recognise, in their case, any connexion between the internal phenomenon—belief, and the external phenomenon—truth. He who, while continuing to recognise the connexion in his own case, refuses to recognise it as existing, *in any degree*, in the case of other men, must do more than assume that he has a *less* share of infirmity than the rest of mankind. He must assume that he is in this respect unique among men. He must assume that, when existing in his mind, belief has a significance which it has not in any other mind. With him—so he must think—belief indicates the presence of objective truth. With the rest of mankind it indicates nothing. I do not imagine that any man would adopt this conclusion when thus nakedly stated; but the denial of all argumentative weight to the general belief of mankind involves no less.

So far, however, we have advanced but a short way. There is little practical utility in the conclusion that *some* argumen-

tative weight ought to be conceded to the belief of mankind, unless we can make some attempt to answer the question—How much? The concession of *some* weight to general belief will avail but little, if the amount conceded is so small that it does not practically affect the question in the decision of which this argument is employed. It is thus that Mr. Mill would treat it:—
"To a thinker," he says, "the argument from other people's opinions has little weight. It is but second-hand evidence; and merely admonishes us to look out for and weigh the reasons on which this conviction of mankind or of wise men was founded."
—*Essay on Theism*, p. 156.

If I rightly understand this passage, the weight which Mr. Mill would allow to the general consent of mankind is very small indeed. If "the argument from other people's opinions . . . . *merely* admonishes us to look out for and weigh the reasons" on which this consent was founded, the word "argument" would seem to be misapplied. If, in the investigation of truth, the history of human belief is to enact a part *merely* suggestive, being allowed no weight in the *final decision* of any question, it is hard to see how the existence of a general belief on any subject could furnish an *argument*, in the proper sense of that word. Such a history will no doubt *suggest* arguments, on which the mind of the inquirer is to decide; but it would seem that no significance ought to be conceded to the mere fact that other men have examined these arguments and believed them to be conclusive. This appears to be the legitimate inference from the passage which I have quoted, although I can hardly think that Mr. Mill intended so sweeping a sentence. If the human mind be not indifferent as between truth and falsehood, some significance must be attached to the fact of human belief. If the human mind *be* indifferent, absolute scepticism seems to be the only attitude which a thinker can assume. The remaining alternative, that each man should attribute to himself a unique power of arriving at truth is, of course, not to be thought of.

But this principle leads us still further. Absolute denial of argumentative weight to the fact of human belief leads, as we have seen, to absolute scepticism. We cannot exclude ourselves from the sentence which we pass on mankind generally. If we deny *all* significance to the fact of human belief, we must deny *all* significance to the fact of our own belief. This is absolute scepticism. If, while we do not absolutely deny it, we pronounce the significance of human belief, considered as an argument, to be very slight, we must pass the same sentence upon the significance of our own belief. This is scepticism too, though not absolute scepticism. In the first case we deny that there is any connexion between the mental phenomenon, belief, and the external phenomenon, objective truth. In the second case, while we do not deny the connexion altogether, we declare that it is very slight. We declare that the number of cases in which this connexion exists exceeds, but only by a very little, the number of cases in which it does not exist; and that, therefore, an argument based upon the assumption of its existence in any particular case is weak, and ought not to be relied on. The first principle would annihilate human knowledge. The second would reduce it to a low probability, to which the term "knowledge" would be quite inapplicable. The effect of either, if logically carried out, would be to remove this word from our vocabulary, or to change its meaning.

But neither principle is logically carried out. Men may deny or underrate the argumentative value of the belief of other men, but they treat their own belief quite differently. It may, indeed, be contended that we *could* not do otherwise. Scepticism with regard to our own belief, it may be said, is impossible, for it involves a contradiction. To realize it, the mind should assume two opposing attitudes at the same moment—at once believing and not believing. It is, then, impossible to carry out the principle logically. A necessity of our nature obliges us to make an exception in our own favour.

I do not here stop to consider the argument against a principle which may be derived from the fact that its logical development is impossible. In the present case I think that the impossibility is only apparent, and that if we were disposed to carry out the principle logically, we could do so. The process, I suppose, would be somewhat of the following kind :—A thinker, who has arrived at the conclusion that no weight ought to be allowed to the belief of other men, finds himself engaged in the investigation of a question. The evidence presented to him is sufficient to produce belief; and as he is probably not thinking at that moment of his general sceptical principle, belief is really produced. Then, however, this principle does occur to his mind. He reflects that he has already condemned as valueless the belief of other men. He has denied that there is any connexion between the internal phenomenon, belief, as appearing in *their* minds, and the external phenomenon, objective truth. Then the thought *may* force its way—What right have I to think that this connexion exists in *my* case? Am I a unique being, whose belief indicates the presence of objective truth, while the belief of every other man is to be regarded as insignificant? Surely this cannot be.

The result of such a train of thought will be to shake the belief which had been produced. It is not that he believes and does not believe at the same moment, but that he ceases to believe—not because the evidence appears to him less convincing than before, but because he has learned to distrust his own faculties. The mind becomes in this instance, and under the influence of the same thought will soon become in every instance, incapable of belief. This is absolute scepticism—a state of mind which is not, as some writers have said, self-contra-

O

dictory. It is not a belief that there is no belief. It is simply incapability of belief. The mind is so changed, that it is no longer capable of producing the phenomenon, belief. I cannot see that there is in this anything self-contradictory, however rare such a state of mind may in reality be. It *is* rare, if indeed it exist at all. Even among those who condemn human belief as worthless, or nearly so, this scepticism is rare, not because they are logical, but because they are illogical—because, while they would discredit the faculties by which other men arrive at truth, they make an unjustifiable exception in favour of their own.

Admitting, however, that a general rejection of the argument derived from human belief cannot be justified by reason, we may still inquire whether we cannot exercise discrimination in the reception of this argument. Are we obliged to assign argumentative weight to every kind of human belief, or are there any which, without *general* scepticism, we are warranted in rejecting? We have seen that belief is an effect which, unless we are prepared to adopt absolute scepticism as the proper attitude of the human mind, we are, in the absence of positive evidence, bound to ascribe to objective truth as its most probable cause. This presumption in favour of truth remains, even in the presence of opposing evidence, and must always be taken into account in estimating the argumentative value of human belief. As, however, this, like all other presumptions, may be overcome by evidence, the first question which, in any case of belief, we must endeavour to determine is, whether there be such evidence—evidence, I mean, not against the truth of the thing believed, but in favour of the existence of a cause of belief other than truth. That there *are* such causes is well known. Early education, self-interest, love, hatred, and others less remarkable, may and do produce belief, in the absence of truth. If the belief in question can be traced with probability to one of these causes, we are justified in attaching proportionately little argumentative weight to such a belief. This probability may often be established when those who join in such a belief have given their reasons for so doing. This statement may show plainly the presence of some one or more of the *extraneous* causes, if we may so call them. The same thing may appear from the arguments by which men seek to win others to their own opinions. If a man try to persuade another to adopt a particular belief, not by laying before him evidence to prove its truth, but by impressing upon him that it is beneficial to himself or others that he should believe it, it is a probable inference that his own belief was influenced by similar considerations. To such a belief we should not be justified in attaching much argumentative weight. It is probably one of those beliefs whose existence is due, not to the truth of the thing believed, but to one of those causes which I have called "extraneous."

We have thus seen that, if the reasons assigned for a certain belief by those who hold it belong to a class which does not profess to be connected with the truth of the thing believed, we are justified in rejecting that belief as devoid of argumentative weight. We have now to inquire whether the same be true in every case in which the reasons appear to us to be insufficient, although professing to belong to a class which *is* connected with the truth of the thing believed. Such appears to be the opinion of Mr. Mill, in the passage already cited, in which he would assign to the fact of human belief a function purely suggestive. If this be its sole function, it is plain that we ought to attach no weight to the fact, that other men have considered these arguments to be conclusive. Is this true ? Ought a thinker, when attempting to determine the force of an argument which other men have examined before him, to leave altogether out of consideration the conclusion at which they have arrived ? Surely such a course would involve the error noticed before—namely, a tacit assumption that his nature is exceptional—that the power of arriving at truth by process of reasoning has been given to him alone. If it have been given in any degree to other men, the rejection of their reasoning as valueless seems to be illogical. The actual amount of weight to be assigned to such reasonings will necessarily depend upon the intellectual power of the reasoners, and upon their freedom from the action of the extraneous causes of belief before alluded to.

It remains to inquire whether any weight ought to be assigned to general belief in truths which come to us not by reason but by intuition. Here it seems to me that a thinker has even less right than in the case of truths obtained by reasoning to set aside as valueless the conclusions of other men. In the case which we have just considered, he may be able to *refute* the arguments on which these conclusions are professedly founded. He may be able to do this so as to satisfy, not only his own mind but also the minds of others, that there is a fatal error in the reasoning employed or in the facts which have been used as premises. He may thus justify his neglect of these conclusions. But an asserted truth which rests immediately on an intuition can neither be proved nor refuted. The acceptance or rejection of such a truth depends on the constitution of the mind to which it is presented, and on nothing else. He who believes it can give no *reason* for his belief beyond this, that he cannot help it. The history of such beliefs cannot, therefore, be *suggestive*, and must be set aside as valueless, if no weight is to be assigned to the mere fact that these beliefs have actually existed. Is such rejection justifiable?

The subject of the supposed intuitive belief is not likely to be a matter of intuition to the thinker himself. Rarely is an intuitive belief displaced from the position which it holds in one man's mind, by his knowledge that it does not hold that position in the minds of other men; and if the beliefs of other men have had any share in implanting the belief in his mind, it cannot be properly called an intuition. But the following observations are applicable to either case.

The answer before given to the proposed rejection of human belief as an argument may be repeated here. Intuitive belief, like any other belief, is a phenomenon to be accounted for. One of the extraneous causes by which other kinds of belief may often be accounted for, namely, fallacious argument, has no place here. If no one of the other extraneous causes, as education, interest, &c., can be with certainty assigned to the phenomenon, we are compelled to allow a certain probability to the theory of this phenomenon, which assigns as its cause the truth of the thing believed. The amount of this probability will necessarily depend on the improbability of the existence and sufficiency of any of the extraneous causes.

Let us take, for example, one of our moral intuitions. It has been observed (let us suppose), that a certain action is very generally condemned by the moral sense of mankind. It is condemned, not on account of any results which may be traced to it, but because the action is regarded as intrinsically bad. But although *generally*, it is not (let us suppose) *universally* condemned. Among those whose moral sense refuses to condemn the action is included the thinker whom we have imagined. Ought he, in such a case, to assign any weight to the fact, that, to the majority of mankind, this action appears bad? Surely this question must be answered in the affirmative. In the absence of the superiority of one class or one individual to the rest, the theory of probabilities would necessarily dispose an impartial judge to give the preference to the conclusion accepted by the greatest number, on the same principle which would lead him to prefer the testimony of a larger number of witnesses to that of a smaller number, in the absence of any proved superiority of the latter in intelligence or truthfulness. Now surely, if the supposed thinker believe, or even suspect, that an impartial judge would decide in this way, he ought not to dismiss as devoid of weight the consent of those who differ from him, even in an intuition.

The argument in favour of the efficacy of prayer derived from the general consent of mankind is, in part though not wholly, of this nature. It is not certainly a mere intuition which makes man a Theist, although it helps to do so. Nor is it from an intuition only that he derives his belief in the efficacy of prayer. Many have learned it, or thought that they learned it, from experience. Many have accepted this, with other revelations of the Infinite, from an authority which they believed to be more than human. But belief in the efficacy of prayer is wider than either of these reasons, and we must seek its cause in that all but universal moral judgment which has decided that indifference to the prayer of a suppliant is inconsistent with the character of a benevolent being. This judgment is not an inference of the reason: it is simply a moral intuition. Those to whose minds it is present can deny its force as an argument only by absolute moral scepticism. Those to whose minds it is not present, if they are not absolute sceptics, can deny its force as an argument only by claiming for their own intuitions a conformity to truth, of which they deny any share to the intuitions of other men. The former alternative involves the surrender of all moral truth; the second is simply absurd.

Before concluding this note, I must notice the objection which Mr. Galton alleges against the argument from general consent. As this question is important, I give Mr. Galton's reasons for rejecting the argument in his own words:—"The argument from universality either proves too much, or else it is suicidal. It either compels us to admit that the prayers of Pagans, of Fetish worshippers, and of Buddhists who turn praying wheels, are recompensed in the same way as those of orthodox believers, or else the general consensus proves that it has no better foundation than the universal tendency of man to gross credulity."[1]

Of this reasoning I have to remark, in the first place, that it gives a very inadequate representation of the argument derived from general consent. This argument is not wholly, nor even chiefly, an argument from experience. It is in great part based on the common element which enters into the Theistic conceptions of all men. That the Supreme Ruler (or Rulers) of the world hears, and to some extent complies with, the expressed desires of men, is perhaps the one point in which all religions agree; and the argument is this—that there is a presumption that the Supreme Being does really possess an attribute with which the moral sense of mankind has universally agreed to invest Him.

But passing by the *à priori* form of this argument, and regarding it as founded solely on experience, we may inquire— What is the absurdity to which Mr. Galton professes to reduce it? It compels us to admit, he thinks, that the prayers of the votaries of false religions are recompensed "in the same way as those of orthodox believers." If by "in the same way" Mr. Galton means "to the same extent," it is plain that we are not required to admit this at all. We do not admit that the experience of all men is of equal value because we admit that the experience of every man is of *some* value. We are not obliged to maintain that the prayers of the Pagan are equally efficacious with the prayers of the Christian, even if we do not deny them all efficacy. But if Mr. Galton's meaning be, that it is absurd to concede *any* efficacy to the prayer of a Pagan, because his religion is untrue, I think that his *reductio ad absurdum* may fairly be disputed.

Every religion which includes the idea of a being higher than

[1] *Fortnightly Review*, ut supra, p. 126.

man, who gives his approval to virtue and his displeasure to vice, includes one true element. It may be combined with a group of false notions which hide its real character; the conception of a Divine Being may be so disfigured by these additions as to seem wholly devoid of truth; and we should probably describe those who had formed it as worshippers of false gods. But this sentence is only partly just. These Theistic conceptions are erroneous, but they are not wholly false; and the question which Mr. Galton's argument requires us to consider is this— Is it absurd to suppose that the Divine Being would have any regard to prayers inspired by a conception of His nature, deeply erroneous certainly, yet not without some elements of truth? When the Red Indian, knowing nothing of Revelation or of Christ, raises his heart in prayer to the Great Spirit whom he thinks of chiefly as the master of the "happy hunting grounds" which are *his* Heaven, is it absurd to suppose that his prayer may meet with a response from God—the God of the Christian? Some might perhaps reply—Yes, it is absurd that such a prayer should be heard by the God of the Christian; for it is not addressed to the God of the Christian—it is addressed to an imaginary being, who has no existence except in the fancy of the worshipper.

In what sense is this proposition true? Let us consider first the case of a non-Christian monotheist. In what sense is it true that the worship of Ormuzd was the worship of an imaginary being? It is not, surely, the *name* which makes him imaginary. If the conception of the Supreme Being formed by the disciple of Zoroaster were identical with the conception of the Supreme Being formed by the Christian, would the prayers of the ancient Persian have been unreal, or the object of his adoration imaginary, because the worshipper chose to call that object Ormuzd? I think not. The difference between a real and an imaginary being must be in something more essential than a name.

Is the object of this worship imaginary because the worshipper's conception of the Supreme Being is erroneous? This argument would prove too much. Passing over the consideration that all human conceptions of the Divine Nature must err, at least by defect, it is enough to remark that even members of the same Christian Church differ so widely in their conceptions of the Divine Nature, that *some* of these conceptions must involve serious error. The God of the Red Indian does not differ more widely from the God of the Christian than the God of the predestinarian differs from the God of the universalist. Yet neither the predestinarian nor the universalist would deny efficacy to the prayers of the other. It may be said, and it is quite true, that these varieties of Christian opinion have in the doctrine of Christ's mediation a common element which separates them from all other forms of belief. But would any Christian pronounce it to be absurd that God should listen to the prayer of a Jew? Why, then, is it to be called absurd that God should listen to the prayer of a Persian?

Mr. Galton's *reductio ad absurdum* is certainly more plausible in the case of a polytheist. Here it may be contended that the conception of the Divine Being which the worshipper has formed contains an element so completely false as to deprive it of all reality. It may be said that of the objects of his worship all but one *must* be imaginary, and that even to that one a worship so divided could not be pleasing. Shall the "jealous God" of the Bible, it may be asked, look with any favour on petitions which He is required to share with Neptune or Ashtaroth?

That such a prayer should meet with the *same* favour as the prayer of the Christian would of course be an absurd supposition. That it meets with any favour at all *may* be an untrue supposition, but it is not absurd. It is not a supposition which we are justified in summarily rejecting, as Mr. Galton proposes to do. Nay, there is even something to be said in its favour. The

P

presence of a Theistic element gives to every system which includes it a certain amount of truth which, so far, distinguishes it favourably from a system in which this element is wanting. No Theist will deny that the polytheist is nearer to the truth than the atheist. Nor does it seem absurd or even improbable that even this approximation to the truth, distant as it is, should meet with some favour in the sight of God. I cannot, therefore, admit the validity of Mr. Galton's *reductio ad absurdum* of the argument from general consent.

There is more truth than theologians generally admit in the Universal Prayer—

"Father of all! in every age,
In every clime adored
By saint, by savage, and by sage,
Jehovah, Jove, or Lord."

If Pope meant that doctrinal differences are unimportant, and that the worship which the Greek or the Roman addressed to Jupiter was *as* true, and therefore *as* pleasing to God, as the worship which the Jew addressed to Jehovah, or the Christian to the Father of our Lord Jesus Christ, he was wrong. But if he meant, as I think he did mean, that pervading all these forms of religion, obscured, but neither destroyed nor even completely hidden by a multitude of false notions, lies one great truth, then he was profoundly right.[1]

Let the Christian value, as highly as he will, the religion which his Master came upon earth to teach. Let him strive, as earnestly as he will, to scatter by the light of that Gospel the clouds of error which rest where its light has never shone. He cannot value it too highly. He cannot strive too hard. But

[1] I may here refer to a a recently published Lecture of Professor Max Müller (*Macmillan's Magazine*, No. 325, pp. 196, *et seq.*), in which he has shown that even in the religions of Central and South Africa there is a closer approximation to the truth than men are generally disposed to admit.

let him not think that he has a monopoly of truth, or that the history of religion shows any exception to the principle, that no system of pure falsehood ever succeeded yet. Falsehood there is indeed abundantly in the religions of the world. The historian of Theism has to tell of portraits of the Divine Nature disfigured by injustice, by selfishness, and by cruelty. Some of these portraits men have drawn for themselves; for some they have professed to find a higher authority. And if, in spite of these hideous caricatures, the historian has to tell that over the whole world Theism has continued to live, it is not to *them* that it owes its vitality. Theism has lived because it *is* Theism; because it contains, undestroyed by all the false notions with which men have associated it, the one true principle, that there is in the universe a Power higher than mere physical force—higher than the forces of the human intellect; a Power which is, or may be, the friend of man, and to which—or may we not say to Whom?—man owes certain duties: obedience always, reverence not quite so generally, love less frequently still. Alas! there have been, and there are, theological systems which would seem to make love impossible. Yet when, possessing even these imperfect glimpses of the truth, man turns to God, as he conceives Him, and asks His aid, must we pronounce it to be an absurdity that the "Father of all" should hear his prayer? God forbid.

THE END.

www.ingramcontent.com/pod-product-compliance
Lightning Source LLC
Chambersburg PA
CBHW031743230426
43669CB00007B/462